ADIRONDAC

D1546000

Alexis de Tocqueville and the New Science of Politics

Alexis de Tocqueville and the New Science of Politics: An Interpretation of *Democracy in America*

John C. Koritansky

Carolina Academic Press
Durham, North Carolina

To my wife, Jeanne

49824

© 1986 by John C. Koritansky
ISBN 0–89089–285–7
Library of Congress Card No. 84–70753
Printed in the United States of America

Carolina Academic Press
P. O. Box 8795 Forest Hills Station
Durham, North Carolina 27707

Contents

Preface

The sole purpose of this book is to elucidate Alexis de Tocqueville's masterpiece, *Democracy in America*. Whatever value it may have will be to the students of that text, most likely in college courses where Tocqueville is a central figure. To say this is to identify my work as one more statement in a vast array of interpretive material that has been written and still is being written on Tocqueville. There seems to be something about both the form and the content of Tocqueville's writing that permits and even facilitates voluminous commentary. Not all of that commentary, however, has dealt with Tocqueville as a political thinker, one from whom we might not only receive information and judgment about Jacksonian America or even democratic society but also to whom statesmen might repair for broad, practical lessons about how to form a democratic citizenry that is strong souled and free. This book belongs to that latter category of interpretive commentary.

What I have written is very much indebted to Marvin Zetterbaum's *Tocqueville and the Problem of Democracy*. That book helped me see what sort of thinker Tocqueville was and it caused me to think that I might understand the controlling purpose of *Democracy in America*. In time, though, I came to doubt the adequacy of what Zetterbaum offers as the solution to the problem of democracy, namely the right understanding of self-interest. It seemed to me more and more clear that, while any successful democracy by Tocqueville's standards would have to accommodate self-interest and would have to cause its citizens to understand self-interest rightly, this whole matter was but one aspect of the entire system of sentiment and belief which finds its summation in civil religion. Having then come to stress civil religion as the core of Tocqueville's practical recommendations, I became more persuaded that Rousseau was the chief philosophical influence on Tocqueville even so that the very definition of freedom as the ultimate aim of Tocqueville's recommendations should be understood in a Rousseau way, as the active involvement in the general will. Finally, it is especially because the real character of civil religion is not always, perhaps not ever, understood by those whom it civilizes that Tocqueville's work bears and requires elucidation.

I am grateful to my colleagues at Hiram College and to the institution for providing an environment where one can do this sort of work. I have enjoyed two summer grants from Hiram College which I used to prepare my articles in *Publius*, summer 1975, and *The Intercollegiate Review*, fall 1976, anticipating some of what appears here. I want to thank Ralph Lerner in particular for the enormous patience he employed years ago in reading and listening to my early attempts to explain Tocqueville and for the relentlessness of his criticism and encouragement. To my teachers, Allan Bloom and Joseph Cropsey, I owe an inexpressable and unpayable debt.

Alexis de Tocqueville and the New Science of Politics

One

How the Emergence of the Idea of Humanity Calls for a New Political Science

In describing his own intention for his book, *Democracy in America*, Alexis de Tocqueville says that he will present a completely "new political science" "for a world itself quite new."[1] Nevertheless, and despite the enormous notoriety of the work, many of those who admire Tocqueville most would be hard-pressed to say just what that new political science is. Tocqueville is generally not accorded the rank he desired among the most eminent students of politics. His book is celebrated for its insights, but seldom is he dealt with as a systematic thinker.

Connected with this is the fact that Tocqueville has stood in good favor with both liberals and conservatives over the years.[2] Conservatives have some reason to count Tocqueville as one of their own, especially for his warning of the dangers of majority tyranny and democratic centralism.[3] If liberals are less prone to adopt Tocqueville as a patron saint, or even fellow traveler, they do tend to respect him for his concern for "individualism" in democracy. Tocqueville's discussion of this point won the attention of John Stuart Mill, and its influence is still observable among such contemporary writers as David Riesman and Charles Reich. But although the themes of centralization and individualism are important to Tocqueville, even central, it remains to be shown how those themes are related to a "new political science," assuming that to mean a new understanding of the nature of political life altogether.

In this book, I will try to describe and evaluate Tocqueville's *Democracy in America* as a comprehensive teaching about politics. Perhaps the best shorthand description of what Tocqueville is trying to do is to say that his *Democracy* has the same breadth of aim as

3

has Montesquieu in the *Esprit des Lois*. It could even be said that Tocqueville is rewriting Montesquieu's work, on the basis of Tocqueville's claim to have discovered that the many different animating principles among the variety of regimes that Montesquieu had studied have been displaced by the one overpowering animus in modern society, i.e., the love of equality. The meaning of the love of equality is the central issue in his work: its roots in human nature, its various forms, its various political consequences, and the latitude it allows to the modern statesman are what Tocqueville tries to illustrate. Almost certainly it was Rousseau who taught Tocqueville to see the root of the love of equality in human nature and to see its centrality for political life. My whole interpretation, then, might be summed up by saying that Tocqueville attempts to rewrite Montesquieu's political science by way of an extension of Rousseau's reinterpretation of human nature.

Among those of Tocqueville's readers who have dealt with him as a systematic thinker are Raymond Aron,[4] Marvin Zetterbaum,[5] Jack Lively,[6] and Seymour Drescher.[7] Aron's essay (in his *Main Currents in Sociological Thought*) makes the valuable observation that Tocqueville follows the example of Montesquieu in recognizing the importance of circumstances of geography and history in his analysis of social life. Modern thinkers earlier than Montesquieu had developed broadly prescriptive social philosophies by thinking through the implications of natural law and the requirements of overcoming the state of nature which is, in its essential characteristics, everywhere the same. Montesquieu's demonstration of the significance of geographical and historical variables in political life causes his prescriptions to be much more subject to qualification. While still intending to be prescriptive, Montesquieu's thought is more heavily descriptive of the actual variation among regimes than that of his predecessors. For this reason Aron cites Montesquieu as a harbinger of modern sociology. Tocqueville represents another step along this same path, for he too operates with Montesquieu's understanding of the way that historical and geographical accidents bear on the question of the regime. The distinction between Tocqueville and Montesquieu is that Tocqueville confines his attention exclusively to democracy, rather than to the entire range of possible or actual regimes. He makes of democracy an ideal type and develops his study of the effects of time and chance only as variations on the same theme. In this way Tocqueville is in one sense more modern than Montesquieu; Tocqueville does not ask us to think seriously about political alternatives that seem to belong to an alien world, known only to historians. In another sense, though, Tocqueville is still quite distinct from the spirit of contemporary sociology because he does not reflect its value neutralism or its demotion of distinctly political questions. Tocqueville is a political thinker like the classical political philosophers in the sense that his task is the identification of the good regime, and the explanation of how, under varying circumstances, it can be approximated.

Aron's discussion of Tocqueville is a statement of Tocqueville's relationship to contemporary sociology as well as to Montesquieu. but, having placed Tocqueville in this set of relationships, Aron scarcely scratches the surface of the *content* of Tocqueville's thought. Having described how Tocqueville "remains closest to classical philosophy, as interpreted by Prof. Leo Strauss,"[8] Aron does not go on to explain why, in substance, Tocqueville is a democratic thinker while classical philosophy rejects democracy. Aron does not show *why* Tocqueville accepts democracy as an ideal. His abstention from his question explains why it was not necessary for him to mention the influence of Rousseau on Tocqueville's thought.

For Seymour Drescher, Tocqueville is important as an interpreter of modernity. Tocqueville's work makes an interesting study because there are two sides of it that represent two different, considered views of what fundamentally determines modern life. The view that characterizes *Democracy in America* is that democracy, or the love of equality, is indeed the basic fact of modernity. But Drescher argues that Tocqueville's more mature view, which he attained as a result of his journey to England, is that industrialization with its consequences is the most important dimension of the future. England replaced America as the model of what the citizens of the world would have to hope for and to fear. For Drescher, only in the final chapter of Book 2 of the second volume of *Democracy in America*, wherein Tocqueville describes the dangers of a new kind of aristocracy being reborn in the modern world as a result of industrial specialization, does he signal his subsequent shift of focus such that America appears to be more an anomaly than an example of the general pattern of the future. Drescher's study is valuable because it does highlight how unique, and even primitive, are the conditions in America. He helps us recognize why the social and political institutions in America cannot serve as examples for Europeans to follow. But there are many indications in the *Democracy* itself that Tocqueville was aware of this fact, and that it does not undermine his contention that in America the most important fact of the modern world is writ in large plain letters as nowhere else. The basic question is whether, in his own final analysis, Tocqueville did not consider England rather than America to be the anomaly, because England is the one Western nation that preserves certain important features of the *ancien régime*. It seems to me that the importance Drescher attaches to the *Journey to England* reflects his own judgment that the analysis presented in *Democracy in America* is unsatisfactory. In the interpretation that follows, I intend to show how Tocqueville could think that *Democracy in America* gives a fully satisfactory account of what the future portends, while understanding in what respects America is primitive.

The approach to Tocqueville that is taken by Marvin Zetterbaum and Jack Lively is the one that promises to get to the heart of his thought. Zetterbaum and Lively recognize Tocqueville to be a *political* thinker, and they set about to lay bare his understanding of the task of modern statesmanship. For them, Tocqueville is a constitutional philosopher like James Madison. Tocqueville does not have the same ideas as Madison regarding the problem he sets forth or the political and social institutions he recommends, but the kind of question that they see Tocqueville raising is the same. My disagreement with Zetterbaum and Lively stems from my view that they do not recognize how much it is the case that the unique circumstances of America renders useless the examples of American institutions as models for European democracy. I argue that, once the importance of circumstances is fully appreciated, Tocqueville's book does not have value as a constitutional philosophy at all; the new science of politics that Tocqueville wishes to teach the modern statesman is more general. Tocqueville thinks that there has been a change in human affairs such that the very nature of political and social life has been altered. He teaches the new nature of common life. The student of Tocqueville's new science of politics is left to figure out the answer to the constitutional question depending on the peculiarities of his own situation.

Zetterbaum's and Lively's reading of *Democracy in America* can be called "conservative" in the following respect. Recognizing the centrality of the love of equality in democracy, they hold that this fact is important because it poses "the problem of democracy" (in Zetterbaum's phrase). They read Tocqueville to have set forth a series of defenses against the corrosive effects of the love of equality. This interpretation derives from Tocqueville's assertion that despotism is at least no less likely in democracy than in the *ancien régime*, and furthermore that in democracy the ancient and traditional barriers to despotism have all been ground to pieces by a process of social atomization. Therefore, say Zetterbaum and Lively, it was Tocqueville's desire to erect new barriers to despotism that do not depend on the old feelings of aristocratic honor, but which are compatible with spiritual and intellectual propensities of democracy. Zetterbaum is especially clear about what Tocqueville hoped would be relied on to build the new barriers to despotism in democracy. The self-interest of the democratic citizens, if it could be a rightly understood self-interest, would animate voluntary associations and provincial governmental units so that they might come to assume the place of traditional barriers to despotism and thus "solve the problem of democracy on the level of democracy." America provides at least the outline of the model to be followed. This interpretation makes Tocqueville a conservative at least in the sense that he is trying to *preserve* a value, freedom, from the ravages of the movement of history.

The interpretation set forth in this book differs from the conservative interpretation because it attaches a positive value to equality itself, and links it more closely with the value of freedom. It must be granted, of course, that democracy may give rise to a certain form of despotism; that is, in fact, Tocqueville's most serious concern. But the despotism to which democracy may give rise is a kind of perversion of democracy's own nature. The equality that is compatible with despotism is always a qualified equality—in the extreme case it is the equality of all men, save one. But the more "legitimate" expression of democratic equality is the equality of all men in freedom. True equality necessarily goes together with freedom, for freedom is the ground and the only ground on which men are all equal. By the same token, true freedom necessarily goes with equality, for freedom is something to which all men, as men, have equal claim.

In the introductory chapter to *Democracy in America*, Tocqueville expresses his famous opinion that the movement of the history of Christendom over the course of the previous 700 years has invariably been in the direction of democratic equality.[9] Every episode in the struggle among competitors for power, every event whatever its immediate purpose or effect, contributed to the overall movement towards the equalization of the social, economic, and political conditions among all men. What he says seems plausible as far as it goes, though it may leave us wondering exactly why the aristocrats of the *ancien régime* had to be caught unawares. Why *could* they not have resisted successfully the rise of the common people?[10] Then, at the conclusion of his brief description of how movements in human affairs all contributed to the spread of equality, he stops his narrative, and as if he were lifting his eyes towards the heavens, he says,

> Everywhere the diverse happenings in the lives of peoples have turned to democracy's profit; all men's efforts have aided it, both those who had no such intention, those who fought for democracy and those who were the declared enemies thereof; all have been driven pell-mell along the same road, and all have worked together, some against their will and some unconsciously, blind instruments in the hands of God.

> If patient observation and sincere meditation have led men of the present day to recognize that both the past and the future of their history consist in the gradual and measured advance of equality, that discovery in itself gives this progress the sacred character of the will of the Sovereign Master. In that case effort to halt democracy appears as a fight against God Himself, and nations have no alternative but to acquiesce in the social state imposed by Providence.[11]

It is possible, of course, to read past this gesture of piety by Tocqueville without much further ado, but would that not be to ignore a possibly valuable hint regarding Tocqueville's value perspective from which he judges the movement of history toward democracy? If the "Providence thesis" *has* any value, it is to suggest that the movement of Western history is progressive. God wills democratic equality, and what God wills is right. This is not to gainsay the future danger of an egalitarian despotism, but it is to say that the idea of freedom in the name of which that despotism is to be resisted is more compatible with the democratic order than with the pre-democratic order. If there was freedom in the *ancien régime*, and Tocqueville says that there was, it was a distorted thing, never properly understood or properly loved as the birthright of all men.

A somewhat closer reading of the "Providence thesis" in the introductory chapter tends to confirm that Tocqueville is revealing his own judgment when he links democracy with the will of God. We can also get an idea of just what Tocqueville means by the word "Providence." Again, when Tocqueville describes, for example, how the struggle between the kings and the nobles redound to the ultimate advantage of the common people, we tend to be persuaded. But the question remains: *why* does democracy win the struggle that it never directly joins? Why are not the common people simply one more element in a protracted struggle for power? To this question, the only explicit answer is, "Providence." But a little before Tocqueville specifically mentions Providence, he delivers the following remark,

> Once the work of the mind had become a source of power and wealth, every addition to knowledge, every fresh discovery, and every new idea became a germ of power within reach of the people. Poetry, eloquence, memory, the graces of the mind, the fires of the imagination and the profundity of thought, all things scattered broadcast by heaven, were a profit to democracy, and even when it was the adversaries of democracy who possessed these things, they still served its cause by *throwing into relief the natural greatness of man.* Thus its conquests spread along with civilization and enlightenment, and literature was an arsenal from which all, including the weak and poor, daily chose their weapons.[12]

Democracy, then, is inevitable in the same way that the spread of civilization and enlightenment are inevitable. The reason that the struggle between the nobles and the kings turned to democracy's advantage is that the human mind was the most powerful tool or weapon to be used in the struggle, and the works of the mind threw "into relief the natural greatness of man." We might say, the idea of humanity itself has come to have a force in human affairs and it is that force that is ultimately irresistible. This impression is confirmed by what Tocqueville says when he speaks of the predemocratic order. In Volume II of the *Democracy*, when Tocqueville is describing the intellectual disposition of democracy, he contrasts the democratic mind with that of antiquity, saying, "The profoundest and most wide-seeing minds of Greece and Rome never managed to grasp the very general but very simple conception of the likeness of all men and of the equal right of all at birth to liberty."[13] Later on, in Volume II, when Tocqueville describes the characteristics of democratic citizens' manners, he again makes his point by way of contrast; this time to one Madame de Sévigné, whom Tocqueville castigates as one who "could not conceive clearly what it was like to suffer if one were not of noble birth."[14] Thus, the people who lived in the pre-democratic order did not attach any importance to the fact that they belonged to a single race—humanity. They did not derive any notion of rights or duties of humanity as such, nor did they feel any attachment to mankind in their hearts. But it seems that once the idea of humanity has made itself felt, its effects can no longer be resisted. One might say that the authority of this idea has a sort of self-evidence that makes it unchallengeable. This interpretation is compatible with the Providence thesis in the suggestion that the idea of humanity is the voice of god working in the souls of men.

But is this idea really new? When Tocqueville makes his uncharitable remark about the "profoundest minds of Greece and Rome," can he have meant to include Cicero, or Plato and Aristotle? How can what Tocqueville says about this account for the prominent fact of Aristotle's definition of man as the "rational animal"? Moreover, if such a recognition of the importance of mind and reason is central to democratic progress, and if the ancients did have that recognition, how can Tocqueville explain why the ancients were not democratic thinkers?

Neither Plato nor Aristotle were democratic thinkers because they understood democracy to assume an equality among the various opinions about justice and the good life; such an assumption was not compatible with their attempt to demonstrate the supremacy of the life of contemplation in the rank of human activities. The monumental discovery of the classical philosophers was that the only activity that is self-fulfilling, and which answers to the human longing for completeness, is that form of thinking that has no particular end or object other than what is simply thinkable. The most strictly drawn consequence of this discovery for political life is that human affairs will be rationally managed only if they are ordered for the sake of contemplation. This is the sense of Plato's famous assertion of the perfect justice of philosophers becoming kings or kings philosophers. Although neither Plato nor Aristotle put forth the idea of philosophical kingship as a practical suggestion, and they suggest rather that there is no political action or at least no publishable program of action whereby the kingship of the philosopher could be brought about, still in some way all of the practical, political writing by Plato and Aristotle and by their devoted students, maintains philosophical kingship as a standard. When Aristotle writes his more democratic books in his *Politics*, he does so as a necessary concession to the factual strength of the "*demos*," and he tries to make the concession as minimal as possible.

Democracy is to be compromised so as to make it susceptible to the influence of those well-bred gentlemen who might be expected to pay their obeisance to philosophy. In rarer but more fortunate circumstances where such concessions are not necessary, aristocracy is to be preferred.[15]

For his part, Tocqueville scarcely acknowledges the existence of the classical political philosophy. He is in no way guided by its political recommendations. The name Aristotle is never mentioned in *Democracy in America*, and Plato is cited, approvingly, only once, as having gained sublimnity for having rejected the doctrine of materialism.[16] Cicero is also mentioned with some reverence, but the main thrust of the reference is that for all his love of republican freedom, Cicero did *not* appreciate the significance of the common heritage of man. Cicero defended Roman liberties with admirable ardor, but he looked impassively upon the Romans' treatment of their enemy captives as worse than beasts.[17] From the perspective of classical philosophy, what is absent from Tocqueville is the idea of contemplation as the activity for the sake of which all other human activities can be directed. Tocqueville does not identify any one activity that is simply and fully human. Therefore, Tocqueville's argument is less satisfying to reason than Plato's on this important point. But the classical idea of what completes human nature is too strict and too restrictive for Tocqueville. From his perspective, it is the classical thinkers who lack something; namely, an idea of humanity that encompasses all human individuals irrespective of their station, including the natural one. By way of summarizing Tocqueville's relationship to classical philosophy, one might way that his interpretation of modern history as driven by the emergence of the idea of humanity assumes the eclipse of the classical idea of human perfection.

Along this way of thinking, Tocqueville appears to have chosen his expression carefully when he says that the works of the mind "[threw] into relief the natural greatness of man." That is to say, the greatness of human nature is not made evident, as in the classical thought, when the essentially human faculty, mind, makes itself its own subject. On the contrary, the greatness of human nature is made evident upon being thrown into relief, as it works upon objects other than itself; and there are a wide variety of possible objects. We express our humanity when we use our intelligence for all sorts of purposes, even though the life of the intelligence is not the highest or most fully human life. In the second volume of the *Democracy*,

Tocqueville says that in man the angel teaches the brute how to satisfy its desires.[18] The thought there is the same as in the introductory chapter; there is a divine element in man which makes him distinctive among the animals, but the divine thing is not the object of our activities. Our gaze is always downward, so to speak, toward the mundane level of our existence. We know our divine natures as a light from above and behind us, and we know it by what it illuminates.

The aim and the importance of all these remarks has been to show that Tocqueville is a thinker in the modern tradition inaugurated by Rousseau. In a letter to Kergolay, Tocqueville confessed his debt to Rousseau as one of the three great influences on his intellectual development, along with Pascal and Montesquieu; and I will demonstrate in this book that the debt to Rousseau was his greatest even among these three. Tocqueville was, of course, not alone in finding Rousseau the great oracle of the idea of humanity. Immanuel Kant wrote a statement of gratitude to Rousseau as a note to his essay on the beautiful and sublime for the same idea.

> I am myself by inclination a seeker after truth. I feel a consuming thirst for knowledge and a restless passion to advance in it, as well as a satisfaction in every forward step. There was a time when I thought that this alone could constitute the honor of mankind, and I despised the common man who knows nothing. Rousseau set me right. This blind prejudice vanished; I learned to respect human nature, and I should consider myself far more useless than the ordinary working man if I did not believe that this view could give worth to all others to establish the rights of man.[20]

Tocqueville's debt to Rousseau was as profound as Kant's, and it is therefore significant that Tocqueville does not take the same turn or arrive at the same conclusion as Kant starting from practically the same point. The important difference between Tocqueville and Kant, and the thinkers who will follow in Kant's train, is that Tocqueville remains, with Rousseau, a *political* thinker, whereas Kant develops an ethical philosophy that makes no place for Tocqueville's political concerns. Kant had derived from the idea of man as rational being a categorical moral imperative, "Act only on a maxim by which you can will that it, at the same time, should become a general law,"[21] or alternatively, "Act so as to treat man, in your own person as well as that of anyone else, always as an end, never merely as a means."[22] Only by obeying the categorical imperative can men express their essentially human ability to choose to govern their behavior by rational principle rather than according to the dictate of some animal want or need. It is a familiar observation that Kant's categorical imperative is a radicalized form of what Rousseau had termed the "general will" in his *Social Contract*. The general will is also a law that must be obeyed by all citizens if they are to be free, for freedom among social beings can exist only when each chooses to do what the generality of the citizens say each must do. However, Rousseau does not go so far as Kant in making the general will a universal moral command, for as he argues, men can be realistically expected to will the general will only in a rather small, tightly structured society in which there is a strict self-censorship and a warm attachment to the particular myths that give the citizens their similar cast of mind. In a word, Rousseau still agrees with Plato on the necessity of a "noble lie" for the maximal unification of the state and the perfection of political life.[23] Kant, on the other hand, because he has made a universal, categorical imperative of the idea of the general will, is against all lying, and with that politics as such becomes a questionable business. On this comparison, Tocqueville is a truer and closer student of Rousseau than is Kant, for he too assumes the posture of a political thinker.

Tocqueville is not only closer to Rousseau than is Kant by reason of the political character of his thinking, but it is tempting to say that Tocqueville is the only writer in the Rousseau tradition who keeps close to the original in this respect. This is explicable with reference to the enormous impact that Kant had on Western thought during the 18th and 19th centuries. Only the "utilitarians" stand in important contrast to Kant as rivals, and they derive from a version of modern thought that predates Rousseau. Even when Kant is transcended by later European thinkers, the political dimension of human life is not taken up again as it had been before. Instead, the new philosophy of history makes political philosophy unnecessary and in a way impossible. The philosophers of history, Hegel and Marx, understood that the categorical imperative makes politics a dubious business; alternatively put, so long as politics is necessary, to act according to the categorical imperative is impossible. If the idea of human freedom has any real meaning, political society must pass away because of its own internal contradictions and yield to a trans-political regime of universal human brotherhood that will mark the culmination of history. Tocqueville never accepted this idea either. In his correspondence with his friend Gobineau, who was studying in Germany, Tocqueville rejected the notion of a philosophy of history as being inimical to men's expressing their freedom through political undertakings.[24] Even though Tocqueville's description of the providential character of Western history towards democracy can be termed quasi-Hegelian and quasi-Marxist, Tocqueville deliberately rejects the idea that history might become a science. For Tocqueville there is, and there will remain, a fundamental ambiguity in the movement of history, despite its identifiable direction. Democracy is compatible either with despotism or with freedom, and it is the ongoing task of statesmanship to determine the difference.

A sign of the political character of Tocqueville's thought is that he regularly addresses himself to a reader that he calls "the legislator"; i.e., he intends to be an instructor for statesmen. In this respect he joins the ranks of Montesquieu and Aristotle. His place among them is unique because he deliberately chooses to operate wholly within the democratic horizon. This qualification does not mean that Tocqueville's political science was deliberately less comprehensive than Montesquieu's or Aristotle's; rather, Tocqueville thought that he understood what earlier political thinkers had not understood: the strength of the idea of humanity that Rousseau had been the one to articulate. Moreover, under the sway of this force in human affairs, man faces the most fundamental and truly most comprehensive alternatives for human life. The new political science for a "world itself quite new" is comprehensive because it deals with the alternative between the most complete form of despotism that the world has ever seen versus the fullest expression of freedom possible for men.

Following his description of the inevitable triumph of democracy and the providential character of that inevitability, Tocqueville sets forth a very general comparison of the *ancien régime* with a democratic order that, he says, "one can imagine" displacing it. The aristocratic order was based fundamentally on the rule of simple force. But once the domination of those who were more powerful had become regularized, "customs and mores . . . set some limits to tyranny and established a sort of law in the midst of force."[25] This social order was not altogether without charm or virtue. Tocqueville observes of it that since the obedience of the serfs assumed the legitimacy of the ruling class, the souls of neither ruler nor ruled were degraded. Moreover, aristocracy exhibited "stability, strength, and above all glory." In contrast, the virtues that democracy seems capable of exhibiting are of a lower but more solid kind.

> At that stage one can imagine a society in which all men, regarding the law as their common work, would love it and submit to it without difficulty; the authority of the government would be respected as necessary, not as sacred; the love felt toward the head of the state would not be a passion but a calm and rational feeling. Each man having some rights and being sure of the enjoyment of those rights, there would be established between all classes a manly confidence and a sort of reciprocal courtesy, as far removed from pride as from servility.
>
> The nation as a body would be less brilliant, less glorious, and perhaps less strong, but the majority of the citizens would enjoy a more prosperous lot, and the people would be pacific not from despair of anything better but from knowing itself to be well-off.[26]

Unfortunately, this happy image does not conform to reality. Democratic citizens have not overcome the weaknesses of pride and ignorance. Tocqueville observes that,

> The breakup of fortunes has diminished the distance between rich and the poor . . . [only to have] provided them with new reasons for hating each other. . . .
>
> The poor have kept most of the prejudices of their fathers without their benefits, their ignorance without their virtues; they accept the doctrine; and self-interest as motive for action without understanding that doctrine; and their egotism is now as unenlightened as their devotion was formerly.[27]

That democracy has not lived up to its brighter prospect should not be surprising. The assumption in the image of democratic society described above is that democratic citizens can come to have so enlightened a sense of their own self-interest, and the social duties that stem from it, that they will have no room in their hearts for the pride that makes men jealous of another's rank even when it is legitimate. But in light of the degree to which that assumption falls short of the facts, we must wonder whether the image of democracy as a society of enlightened animals is not unrealistic even as a model. Men have not overcome their pride merely because they no longer can enjoy the satisfactions of pride aristocracy made avail-

able, and in the light of that fact, the picture of democracy as a
society of people animated wholly by an innocent and rational self-
preference must appear naive. In any case, Tocqueville refuses to
join those who would seek to improve and purify democracy by
exhorting democratic citizens to think and act upon their own self-
interest. In fact, Tocqueville scorns those,

> whose object is to make men materialists, to find out what is
> useful without concern for justice, to have science quite without
> belief and prosperity without virtue. Such men are called the
> champions of civilization, and they insolently put themselves at
> its head, usurping a place which has been abandoned to them,
> though they are utterly unworthy of it.[28]

It seems that the picture of democracy as a society where enlightened men pursue only their material well-being is not only unrealistic but also ugly. It is ugly and unrealistic for the same reason—
it rests on an incomplete account of the needs of human nature.

In contrast with the materialists, Tocqueville finds himself of
more kindred spirit with Christians. These men, perhaps just because they do not reduce the human soul to the operation of matter
in motion, are ready to "espouse the cause of human liberty as the
cause of all moral greatness."[29] Christianity ought to find itself
compatible with democracy, since "Christianity, which has declared
all men equal in the sight of God, cannot hesitate to acknowledge
all citizens equal before the law."[30] But because the false champions
of modernity have linked democracy with materialism, Christianity
has conceived itself to be in league with the *ancien régime*, with the
result that the men of nobler sentiments do not give their attention
to democracy's improvement but rather try to resist it. The improper
alliance between Christianity and the *ancien régime* has caused those
who are the partisans of democracy to disavow religion, and to
endorse a materialistic account of human life even though their
moral sense inclines otherwise. Those who are the most venal element among mankind are thought of by themselves and others as
the prototype of the citizens of the future.

> Where are we then? Men of religion fight against freedom, and
> the lovers of liberty attack religions; noble and generous spirits
> praise slavery, while low servile minds preach independence; hon-
> est and enlightened citizens are the enemies of all progress, while

> men without patriotism or morals make themselves the apostles
> of civilization and enlightenment![31]

Tocqueville says that this situation is so perverse that it is impossible to imagine that it is to this end that God has guided the destiny of the past seven hundred years of Western history. The modern world is highly unstable. But while the confusion exists, men cannot see clearly what sort of new political science is needed to improve and purify democracy in the way that it can be improved and purified. The key to the confusion of the modern mind is the link between modernity and materialism, and the acceptance of that link by the men of religion. Tocqueville's new science of politics will have to be keen where the picture of democracy that "one can imagine" is naive. Despite the fact that democracy will always be less brilliant and have less to offer by way of glory than aristocracy, some form of satisfaction for men's pride will have to be found that does conform to the democratic social condition. Because democracy will never be able to count on the sort of blind devotion to authority that marked aristocratic order, it will have to find some way of appealing to men to transcend their own self-interest and to act for the sake of a larger good. If freedom is to be preserved in modern democracy, some means will have to be found to elicit the love of freedom for its own sake rather than for its supposed material benefits. Democratic man's pride will not only have to be accommodated, it will ultimately have to be relied upon as the source of that irrational spiritedness that can cause a man to choose liberty over life itself.

Tocqueville says he studied democracy in America to find "lessons from which we might profit."[32] America has lessons to offer because the creative source of laws and mores is the same in the two countries, America and France. America also presents the example of an even more unqualified democracy than France, for in America there is scarcely a remnant of any anti-democratic element. Tocqueville warns against taking his description of the institutions and other features of American democracy as models for French or European regimes to imitate. He is "very far from believing that [the Americans] have found the only form possible for democratic government."[33] American institutions cannot be successfully imitated in Europe because America has been spared the most severe form of weakness to which democracy is subject. The petty and waspish jealousy that Tocqueville complained of as the great vice of contemporary European democracy is not as great a problem in America for two related reasons. First, America is the land of boundless opportunity for individual initiative. The continual and restless desire among democratic citizens to vindicate their notion of their own self-importance does not lead them directly to the jealousy and hatred of others as it tends to in Europe. Second, America has been taken over by the democratic passion without a struggle. The old class antagonisms are a kind of distant rumor in America rather than a memory that is, as in France, still no more than one generation old. To the extent that America does exemplify a well-governed democracy, its success depends critically upon unique and fortunate circumstances that cannot be reproduced elsewhere. The point here is a subtle one, and one of the chief difficulties of any interpretation of Tocqueville's book on democracy in America is to sort out in just what respects the examples that Tocqueville discusses of American institutions are inapposite to Europe because of the peculiarity of American circumstances. Tocqueville suggests that America's success is not entirely due to its circumstances, for there are other nations similarly situated that fail where America succeeds because they lack its institutions; but at the same time America's fortuitous circumstances are an indispensable element in the explanation of how those good institutions actually work. Many of America's institutions simply may not work in France, and even those that might be useful will require additional support to protect them against the ravages of the more destructive form of democratic forces that are less dangerous in America. What America has accomplished depends critically upon luck, and what luck has done for America, the art of Tocqueville's "legislator" will have to do for France.

Near the end of Tocqueville's statement that he wishes his description of America to be useful, he delivers a remark which has become famous, one to be occasionally repeated throughout the book, that he "has not even claimed to judge whether the progress of the social revolution which I consider irresistible, is profitable or prejudicial for mankind."[34] In what sense can Tocqueville intend this statement? How can Tocqueville maintain reservations about the ultimate rightness of democracy when he has already asserted that its triumph must be interpreted as a providential fact, and that to fight against it is to fight against civilization itself as well as the will of God? Many of Tocqueville's readers have concluded from this and similar expressions that Tocqueville was never fully able to overcome his taste for the splendors of aristocratic society, even knowing them to be passé. In this view, the ultimate comparison between aristocracy and democracy is between brilliance and glory versus broadly shared prosperity, and in the final analysis justice; and although he knew he must nod to and serve the new order, he could not help his nostalgic feelings about the past. His sober mind had mastered a reluctant heart, but not without wounding it.[35] This view is plausible; and in one respect Tocqueville does say explicitly, in his discussion of the much stricter standards of politeness in the pre-democratic age, that "it is permissible to regret," the passing of one feature of the aristocratic way of life. Nevertheless, the image of Tocqueville resigning himself to a grey duty but still pining for the splendor of an earlier age is, I suggest, overdrawn. Even in the context of his deferential statement about aristocratic etiquette, he admits that "One should not attach too much importance to this loss."[36] When we try to judge what were Tocqueville's deepest feelings about aristocracy, surely his savage remarks about the inhumanity of Madame de Sévigné must be borne in mind, and Tocqueville knows that her attitude is inseparably linked to what essentially is lacking in the pre-democratic order. If it were in truth the case that Tocqueville continued to feel in his heart that the condition of human life was richer in pre-democratic ages, why does he counsel that we should submit to the ways of the future, however irresistible? Is there not an especially sweet form of grandeur in defending a noble cause that is lost?

I suggest that the reason Tocqueville refuses to judge whether democracy's inevitable triumph is profitable or prejudicial is not because he has moral or even sentimental qualms about the loss of aristocratic glories, but because he cannot defend democracy by demonstrating its compatibility with a definitive view of human perfection. Tocqueville has thought through the implications of his denial of the relevance of any definite statement of the aim of human life whereby perfection might be attained. He is, I think, aware that no such formal defense could be successful. As Aristotle had demonstrated in his *Politics*, any positive statement of a standard or criterion of human perfection leads to the consequence that the one who is best in that regard ought to rule.[37] If there is no identifiable one who is best, then those few ought to rule who give the closest approximation to whatever is taken to be the standard. Any case for democracy therefore depends upon a neutrality towards the issue of human perfection, so that democracy can only win the contest by default, so to speak. That Tocqueville cannot judge whether democracy's triumph is ultimately prejudicial or profitable is, one might say, an indication of the democratic disposition of his mind, and he is aware of it as such.

Tocqueville seeks to improve democracy by causing it to be compatible with freedom. He seeks to improve democracy by bringing out what is democracy's own implicit value. For, in essence, democracy is the dim but massively powerful perception of "the equal right of all men at birth to liberty." It is because democracy does have a certain instinctive love of liberty that Tocqueville confesses his own attachment to it.

> I admire the way it insinuates deep into the heart and mind of every man some vague notion and some instinctive inclination toward political freedom, thereby preparing the antidote for the ill which it has produced. That is why I cling to it.[38]

Thus, Tocqueville believes in the rightness of democracy as a consequence of his own fervid love of freedom. His statement that he cannot judge whether democracy is profitable or prejudicial for mankind is ultimately derivative from the ambiguity in the idea of freedom itself —and Tocqueville is aware of this ambiguity despite his devotion to freedom. An indication of this is his statement at the very end of the introductory chapter:

> It must not be forgotten that an author who wishes to be understood is bound to derive all the theoretical consequences from each of his ideas and must go to the verge of what is false or impracticable, for while it is sometimes necessary to brush rules of logic aside in action, one cannot do so in the same way in conversation, and a man finds it almost as difficult to be inconsequent in speech as he generally finds it to be consistent in action.[39]

What Tocqueville says in this curious passage is something more than that we must sometimes act on the basis of less than complete information and less than fully persuasive reasons. He says literally that there is a disjunction between the realm of rational discourse and the realm of action and that the deficiency lies in the realm of rational discourse. The standard that controls Tocqueville's judgment has a decisive bearing on the realm of actions, but it cannot be successfully articulated. When Tocqueville says that he cannot judge whether democracy is ultimately prejudicial or profitable for mankind, I suggest that he means that he is attached to democracy by that self-same feeling for the equal right of all men at birth to liberty that, however dimly, animates the hearts of modern men. He is, however, under no illusion that he can articulate a defense for that feeling.

Throughout his life, from the enormous success that greeted him upon publication of the first volume of *Democracy in America* to his last years of disappointment and despair for the political future for his native and beloved France, Tocqueville remained steadfastly devoted to freedom, and just as steadfastly cognizant that the object of his chief devotion was a thing that defied rational grasp. In his *Ancien Régime*, the book written during his more mature years, he asserts openly and boldly that the love of freedom is the irrational passion that is the source of everything great. Speaking generally of nations that have lost their freedom, he says,

> It is easy to see that what is lacking in such nations is a genuine love of freedom, that lofty aspiration that, I confess, defies analysis. For it is something that one must *feel* and logic has no part in it. It is a privilege of noble minds which God has fitted to receive it, and it inspired them with a generous fervor. But to meaner souls, untouched by the sacred flame, it may well seem incomprehensible.[40]

It is this same spirit that we find permeating all the institutions and the features of American life guided by Tocqueville's skillful description. To perceive that spirit we must learn to see with Tocqueville's eyes. For Tocqueville sees more of the Americans than they see of themselves. The Americans *are* a great people, but are almost unaware of their common life as a people. The Americans *are* animated by a love of freedom; a deep and powerful passion, but one might almost say an unconscious one. Without exhortation, and writing with a subtlety that will be understood by "the legislator," Tocqueville reveals what must be elevated to the consciousness of European democracy to make free institutions work there. Tocqueville calls for a structuring of democratic society and for a poetic description so that the citizens of modern democracy may feel their involvement in their national life, and come within reach of the passionate devotion to political freedom that may redeem the modern world.

Two

Governmental Institutions:

Volume I, Part I

The first volume of *Democracy in America* derived much of its almost instant notoriety from its elaborate discussion of the complex American scheme of governmental institutions and administrative decentralization.[1] Nevertheless, this same section of the book is probably the least well read part of Tocqueville's work today. The reason for this is natural enough; Tocqueville's European audience would be keenly interested in a description of contemporary American institutions. Montesquieu had demonstrated the utility of studying the actual various forms of political constitution towards discovering general principles of political science, and Tocqueville was recognized as writing in that tradition. America was looked to by Frenchmen as an experiment in democracy; Tocqueville's assertion that he sought useful lessons for Europe in America could be counted on to stike a receptive ear particularly when he described the arrangement of governmental institutions. Today's reader, on the other hand, is inclined to pass over the material in the first part of Volume I hurriedly, precisely because it is hard to imagine that what Tocqueville describes of the workings of American institutions in 1825—especially his account of the separation of powers and local political and administrative discretion—would still have much relevance in the changed circumstances in which we live. To the extent that it is paid much attention, Tocqueville's discussion is often appreciated as primarily a brief for provincial liberties and administrative decentralization. In this section Tocqueville emerges as the great herald of the danger of the "centralizing passion" in democracy. But even though the issue of decentralization is by no means unimportant today, we hardly expect that the description of the specific arrangements by which centralization is resisted that Tocqueville provides could still be informative now that the nation as a whole has grown smaller, and more populous, and the involvement of government in our lives has increased. Nevertheless, I hope to show that Tocqueville's discussion of American governmental institutions still has its original importance, despite the changes in our circumstances.

The difference between the circumstances of contemporary America and America in 1825 is important in the same way that the difference between nineteenth-century America and nineteenth-century France is important. Tocqueville never intended the complicated federal structure of America to serve as a model for other nations to copy. At the end of Part I of Volume I Tocqueville says that the defects of the American federal system of government are the complicated means that it employs and the comparative weakness of the central government; and he asserts that therefore it would simply not do for a nation where the requirements for a strong and efficient central administration were greater. It is especially important that America does not have to be prepared for war in the way that other nations must be.

> Generally speaking, then, it is war which most obviously and dangerously reveals the weakness of a government, and I have shown that the inherent defect of federal governments is to be very weak.
>
> No one can appreciate the advantages of a federal system more than I. I hold it to be one of the most powerful combinations favoring human prosperity and freedom. I envy the lot of the nations that have been allowed to adopt it. But I refuse to believe that, with equal force on either side, a confederated nation can long fight against a nation with centralized governmental power. A nation that divided its sovereignty when faced by the great military monarchies of Europe would seem to me, by that very act, to be abdicating its power, and perhaps its existence and its name.[2]

The unique circumstances of nineteenth-century America as Tocqueville describes them are so important that it would not be an exaggeration to say that Tocqueville means his description of American institutions to demonstrate what will *not* work elsewhere, although this would be an oversimplification. In this discussion Tocqueville reveals why we must search for substitute means.

In chapter 1 of the book Tocqueville describes the physical circumstances of American democracy with a kind of fascination. He explains how America lay before the first White settlers, openly bountiful. The North American continent is one enormous valley, watered by a mighty but gentle river. Within that valley the limits to what one might acquire are set only by the limits of one's imagination and physical strength. Even though at the time of Tocqueville's writing most Americans still lived east of the Alleghenies, it was in the West where the real future of the nation lay. As Tocqueville describes them, the Americans were like a people perched in readiness to enter their own promised land.[3]

The important consequence of what Tocqueville says about the physical circumstances of America is that the effects of democratic jealousy are much less severe in America than they are in Europe. This is so for two related reasons. First, given the almost unlimited opportunity to pursue one's own fortune relying on one's own strengths, it is not so necessary that men seek to gain at one another's expense. Students of James Madison's Federalist no. 10 might reflect that Madison's hope to defuse the "leveling spirit" by a system of government that relies upon the private pursuit of self-interest has a greater degree of plausibility in America because of the conditions that Tocqueville describes. Second, the openness of the American continent makes the establishment of a landed aristocracy almost impossible.[4] Permanent social inequality rests on the forceful control of scarce resources, generally land, by a few, and in America no such permanent control is imaginable. A democratic social condition came naturally to the Americans; they never had to win their social equality from a pre-established social class. The egalitarian idolatry that persists as a result of the memories of the war between the classes in France is at most only potentially present in America. This fact has a decisive significance for the success of the American system of government.

Tocqueville includes a description of the American Indians in his account of the physical circumstances of American democracy. He describes them as living in a condition of both equality and freedom, but it is neither the equality nor the freedom of free and equal citizens. On the contrary, the Indians lived in barbarous independence of one another; they scarcely had any social duties at all. Tocqueville says that the Indians "were untroubled by those muddled and incoherent concepts of good and evil and by that deep corruption which generally mingles with roughness and ignorance among once civilized peoples relapsed into barbarism. The Indian owed nothing to anybody but himself; his virtues, vices, and prejudices were all his own; his nature had matured in wild freedom."[5] Despite their freedom and equality, the Indians could not be said to have lived in a democratic social condition. Tocqueville observes a strong similarity between the Indians and medieval European aristocracy. Both the Indian and the feudal noble honored the same pursuits, war and hunting, and they both had the same aversion to labor rooted in overweening pride.[6] Later, in the final chapter of Volume I, Tocqueville develops this theme further, and he reveals the connection between the irresistible doom that faces the Indian way of life and the inevitibility of democracy itself.[7] But for the present he refrains from describing the Indians' unhappy future. Rather, he depicts a romantic picture of an almost noble savage, whose independence and innocence is a delicate flower. The Indian appears to represent the childhood of mankind. He enjoyed a freedom that can never be regained—nor is it clear that we wish it could be; and yet somehow we revere the Indian in the naturalness of his freedom. Just as it was for Rousseau, the political freedom that Tocqueville tries to support has a more original counterpart in the pre-civilized condition of man.[8]

Tocqueville's description of the physical conditions of American democracy is crucial, but only as a limiting consideration. It is only when he turns his attention to the Whites, in the second chapter, that Tocqueville lays bare the formative principles of American democracy. Of this chapter Tocqueville goes so far as to say that it contains "the germ of all that is to follow."[9] It is in Puritan New England where the political virtues that characterize the United States originated. As for the southern states, Tocqueville simply says that they were settled by mere adventurers, "seekers after gold," and they therefore did not give sufficient care to the formation of their political communities. The gravest evil that was tolerated in the south was the introduction of slavery. In the final chapter of Volume I, Tocqueville explains his thought that this one factor, slavery, will spell the collapse of the southern civilization. At this point, however, Tocqueville only wishes to draw a sharp contrast between the southern colonists and the settlers of "the English colonies of the North, better known as the states of New England, [in which] the two or three main principles now forming the basic theory of the United States were combined."[10]

In contrast to the southerners, the Puritans "tore themselves away from home comforts in obedience to a purely intellectual craving; in facing the inevitible sufferings of exile they hoped for the triumph of *an idea*."[11] The idea for which these men sacrificed everything was, it should be noted, not that of republican government nor any political principle they might have learned from England. Rather their idea was Puritanism itself which, Tocqueville says, was both a religious and a social-political doctrine. The New England fathers wanted to construct a city on a hill that would stand as a model community for Christians to emulate. This dedication engendered throughout the Puritan communities a vigorous public spirit that is reflected in their incredibly harsh criminal code, which they have simply taken from Exodus, Leviticus, and Deuteronomy. It is not for the content of that criminal code that the New England fathers deserve praise; indeed, Tocqueville describes those criminal provisions as being the work of "a rough and half-civilized people."[12] It is, rather, the level of public spirit required to pass and to bear gladly such legislation that arrests Tocqueville's attention.

> Nothing is more peculiar or more instructive than the legislation of this time. . . . The Connecticut lawgivers turned their attention first to the criminal code and, in composing it, conceived the strange idea of borrowing their provisions from the text of holy writ: "If any man after legal conviction shall have or worship any other God but the Lord God, he shall be put to death."[13]

This passage is followed by a description of laws that impose terrible penalties for what seem to the modern reader to be relatively light offenses; but the content of these laws is only incidentally important for Tocqueville. His main concern is to show that "these ridiculous and tyrannical laws were voted by the free agreement of all interested parties themselves." These were free men.

> Alongside this criminal code so strongly marked by narrow sectarian spirit and all the religious passions, . . . was a body of political law, which, though two hundred years ago, still seems far in advance of the spirit of freedom in our own age.[14]

Political freedom stood side by side with the ridiculous and tyrannical laws, and these two things actually nourished each other. The harshness of their laws was the expression of these men's religious zeal, and it was that very zeal that fired their spirit and made them free.

> Clearly they had a higher and more comprehensive conception of the duties of society toward its members than had the lawgivers of Europe at that time, and they had imposed obligations upon it which were still shirked elsewhere....
>
> All the general principles on which modern constitutions rest, principles which most Europeans in the seventeenth century scarcely understood and whose dominance in Great Britain was then far from complete, are recognized and given authority by the laws of New England; the participation of the people in public affairs, the free voting of taxes, the responsibility of public officials, individual freedom, (!) and trial by jury—all these things were established without question and with practical effect.[15]

In saying that the New England Puritans were free although they enjoyed practically no private liberty, Tocqueville is expressing his judgment in favor of Rousseau's redefinition of the meaning of freedom as against what freedom meant for James Madison, or John Locke and the other founders of the classical liberal tradition. The difference is important. For Rousseau, and for Tocqueville, freedom is not what a private individual retains when he submits to a limited authority. Freedom is not opposed to obedience; on the contrary, Tocqueville accepts the newer idea that freedom consists in obedience to self-made law. That obedience is, as Rousseau said, not freedom from the authority of civil society but freedom in civil society. It is the active participation in the general will. Freedom of this sort can be nourished by the sort of zeal that the harsh and totalitarian laws of early New England reflect because freedom of this sort required absolute dedication to the common good as if it were the comprehensive human good. This chapter contains the "germ" of what follows if we read Tocqueville's subsequent description of American political institutions, and his description of the propensities of the ruling element in democracy, to showing how, under a different expression, the essential spirit of freedom of Puritan New England survives in nineteenth-century America.

In chapters 3 and 4 Tocqueville describes the social state of the Americans and the political consequences that they derive from that social state. The main point that he makes about the Americans' social condition is that democracy works a sort of atomizing effect.[16]

While it is true that there exist differences among individuals in wealth, those differences are tolerated only because they do not seriously qualify the essential interchangeability of American citizens. No individual has any particular significance except as a citizen of the democratic community. The atomization of society is an inexorable fact of democratic institutions and laws, the leading example of which is the law abolishing primogeniture. In fact, the abolishment of primogeniture has a key role in the explanation of democracy's inevitability because it " . . . divides, shares, and spreads property and power; . . . "[17] Sometimes people become frightened of these effects and seek to reverse them, "But all in vain! It grinds up or smashes everything that stands in its way; with the continual rise and fall of its hammer strokes, everything is reduced to a fine, impalpable dust, and that dust is the foundation of democracy."[18] Tocqueville observes that in the American west, where this process has gone the farthest, it is as if a person had no past nor any future that would give his individual existence any special significance. In that respect, the west demonstrates the future of all democratic societies however organized.

While the example of democratic "social" condition that the Americans present leaves no room for qualification, the political consequences that might be produced by those social conditions are ambiguous. The individuals who have been reduced to interchangeable particles of dust by democracy can either form themselves into a collectivity that rules its own affairs, or they can submit to an absolute despotism. Democracy can either exhibit popular sovereignty as a genuinely active principle, or can become a dead letter under the cover of which an absolute despot works his own will. This set of political alternatives is linked to an intellectual and emotional alternative in the disposition among democratic citizens that Tocqueville sets forth in the following way.

> There is indeed a manly and legitimate passion for equality which rouses in all men a desire to be strong and respected. This passion tends to elevate the little man to the rank of the great. But the human heart also nourishes a debased taste for equality, which leads the weak to want to drag the strong down to their level and which induces men to prefer equality in servitude to inequality in freedom.[19]

America deserves to be studied because the Americans are animated by the manly and legitimate passion for equality, and they do make the principle of popular sovereignty practically effective. "Sometimes the body of the people makes the laws, as at Athens; sometimes deputies, elected by universal suffrage, represent it and act in its name under almost its immediate supervision."[20] Tocqueville turns, in the remainder of Part I of the first volume (chapters 5–8), to the question of how the degree of active popular involvement in their own self-government can be sustained among a people who occupy a territory as vast as the United States.

The manly and legitimate form of the love of equality that animates the truly popular sovereignty is possible only in a small regime. In a large regime the democratic passion could not but take its less noble form; it would become a desire for a sort of dead level material and social equality. Personal distinction and inequality in terms of public recognition for personal merit *can* be bestowed by a political community that knows it shares the most important things in common. But where there is no real community, where the citizens do not understand themselves to share any common life or common project, then only the semblance of equality—i.e., the equality of private holdings —can be attained. But the irony of the democratic passion is that it itself tends to destroy the conditions under which it can take its noble form. Large nations, Tocqueville affirms, are the incontrovertable fact of the future. Sheer military necessity mitigates against the possibility of a small republic in a world of large nations. Only if the whole world were broken up into a myriad of little regimes would any one of them be able to retain its independence. But such a picture of the world is naive; it is the picture of a barbaric anarchy in human affairs and it is for that reason unmindful of the force of history in the direction of democratic civilization.

The free Puritan communities Tocqueville described in chapter 2 are inconceivable in modern times. Their "crude and half civilized" law code was suitable only so long as they had the good fortune to exist "in solitude." The ironical fact is that the very democratic passion that we observe in so vigorous a form in Puritan New England is harmful to the political conditions under which that passion can take its noble form. The love of equality tends to break down the limiting horizons of the small regime; its instinct is that all men should live by one law, and unless instructed to the healthy limits of its instinct, democracy tends to impose the rule of its own law as far as the collective strength of the community can take it.

Given this self corrupting character of the love of equality, Tocqueville described local freedom to be like a precious but primitive flower. Only in the almost miraculous conditions of America has it survived the maturation of democracy, and it is hard to imagine how it might take root once its requisite conditions have passed.

> ... Hence, until communal freedom has come to form a part of mores, it can easily be destroyed, and it cannot enter mores without a long-recognized legal existence.
>
> So communal freedom is not, one may almost say, the fruit of human effort. It is seldom created, but rather springs up of its own accord. It grows, almost in secret, amid a semi-barbarous society. The continual action of its laws, mores, circumstances, and, above all, time may succeed in consolidating it. Among all the nations of continental Europe, one may say that there is not one that understands communal liberty.[21]

In order to account for the fact that Tocqueville's thought is not hopelessly pessimistic when taken as a whole, it is necessary to observe and to underscore that he says communal freedom is "seldom" created. Were it never to be able to be generated or regenerated in a mature democracy, the future of democratic Europe would be without hope. For there is no substitute for local freedom; citizens cannot learn the meaning of democratic freedom other than through its active expression.

> Local institutions are to liberty what primary schools are to science; they put it within the people's reach; they teach the people to appreciate its peaceful enjoyment and accustoms them to make use of it. Without local institutions a nation may give itself a free government, but it has not got the spirit of liberty.[22]

Tocqueville's description of the contemporary New England towns in chapter 5 reveals that the spirit of liberty was still active in them. Perhaps the most notable point of that description is that the towns were not governed through elective officers but rather that the people itself assembled to dispose of their local business.[23] But how is this provincial freedom preserved? This question provides the significance for Tocqueville's whole discussion of the complex American scheme of government.

If anything of the virtues of the small regime is to be preserved in the modern world some sort of federal union or "decentraliza-tion" is required. The difficulty here, however, is that the same democratic instinct that makes large nations necessary also tends in the direction of simple government and legislative supremacism. In Part I of the first volume of the *Democracy* Tocqueville is con-cerned with legislative supremacism as *the* overriding problem. In America it is particularly the state legislatures that Tocqueville treats as the locus of the tendency towards democratic centralism. State governments are the locus because the state governments are the ones in which are vested the general powers of government that touch peoples' everyday lives; the federal powers are, in contrast, strictly limited and are the exception rather than the rule.[24]

The legislature tends to be supreme because, strictly speaking, legislative supremacy is a necessary implication of democracy. Toc-queville observes that the legislative power is the "authority which springs most directly from the people, it is also that which shares its all-embracing power most."[25] Not only is the legislature most directly responsible to the people, but even more importantly, the legislative function corresponds to the kind of political activity the people themselves would perform if they actually assembled. There can be no rebuttal of the literal supremacy of the legislative power compatible with democracy. But the important practical question that remains is how far, or to what degree of detail is the exercise of the legislative power to extend?

Legislative supremacy is in legal form and appearance the closest thing to direct popular rule; therefore not only is legislative supremacy essential to democracy but democracy also tends in the direction of a simple rule of law unimpeded by any perception of the need for administrative discretion or provincial autonomy. Any argument that limits the ability of the law to govern every last detail of human life involves some allegation of complex circumstances that need special, particular accomodation. But democracy is im-patient with such claims. The image that corresponds most closely to the democratic vision is that of social atomism; the atoms them-selves are perfectly simple and interchangeable and a few majestic generalities govern them suitably. Democratic citizens always suspect the allegation of special circumstances to be a cover for inequality, and in a way the suspicion is always correct.

Is there a way of somehow preventing or qualifying the con-solidation of government consistent with the love of equality? We should not expect that democratic men will ever have an affection for local freedom that displaces their passion for equality. It is necessary to generate some sort of provincial liberty that is compatible with that passion. Can the equality of all citizens be understood in a way that permits local freedom? Strictly speaking the answer is yes, for the notion that in cases where the general public is not necessarily concerned the individual should judge for himself is a corollary of political equality, and it can be used to defend local as well as personal liberties. Even though democracy may not be led to this principle by following its own instincts, Tocqueville thinks it might be made palatable.[26] Still, even if democracy does accept the idea of provincial liberty in a general way, it is still highly questionable whether it will be able to apply the principle and profit from it is specific cases, because the question of which cases the general publlc need be concerned about is ambiguous. There is no simple, legally formulated answer to this question, and whatever is defended as salutary local freedom is open to the charge of being a shoddy cover for the defense of advantages for some.

As a demonstration of the difficulty of this problem, Tocqueville advances a distinction in principle between two different kinds of centralization, political and administrative, only to show its ambiguity in practice. It would seem that it we could educate democracy in this distinction, then we could satisfy democracy's passion for centralization while maintaining the advantages of the right kind of decentralization. Unfortunately the distinction between political and administrative decentralization is not clear, nor is it clear whether the duplication of merely "ministerial" activities will school democracy in the matter of political responsibility or meaningful freedom. Tocqueville cites the distinction as deriving from "certain interests, such as the enactment of general laws and the nation's relations with foreigners, [that] are common to all parts of the nation, [as distinct from] other interests of special concern to certain parts of the nation, such, for instance, as local enterprises."[27] But even this rather vague distinction is rendered questionable by the concurrent admission that "there are some points where the two sorts of centralization become confused,"[28] and that "order even in secondary affairs is a national interest."[29] There must be uniformity—unity— in matters that concern the nation *per se, but which matters are those?*

The interpretation of this provision most friendly to local liberty is that unity of command is a necessity where the existence of the community itself is at stake, to marshall the whole force of the community in defense against an enemy. Thus understood, political centralization would require only a unity of command in an independent executive charged to preserve and protect the community. All other matters: public welfare, regulation of the economy, education, are such as can, conceivably, be addressed at the level of local government. Such a community, however, would be held together only so long as the agent of the sovereign were sufficiently powerful. The differences in manners and currency, for example, would tend to destroy the community. Indeed Tocqueville thinks that such divergences as do exist among the different states of the union will cause it to break apart.[30]

Uniformity is necessary beyond that unity of command which, in the strictest view, is a matter of the whole community's concern. But how much? When is there a need for uniformity in general regulation? Does the public school system require central administration? the police force? fire prevention or waste disposal? What of regulatory matters, zoning, health and safety legislation, wage and hour legislation? The answer to the question in any one of these instances is an answer that "depends." It depends on an assessment of the inconvenience of non-uniformity among localities, on one hand, measured against the incremental effect of this particular restriction of the local communities' prerogatives on the capacity of the local community to interest its citizens and teach them the limits of self-government. There is no possibility of an *a priori* resolution of this issue. Each case is a judgment call. The only conclusion is that the need for administrative decentralization to civilize democracy is a need for constant wise judgment—for "living wisdom."

The reliance upon the institutionalization of "living wisdom" is the reason Tocqueville devotes as much attention as he does to the Courts of Sessions and particularly the office of justice of the peace. The justices of the peace are rather special men in a special situation. They are the tribunal for administrative officers; they ensure that local officials perform their legal duties. Although these men are charged by the state to ensure the rule of law, they are not simply men of the law. They are, more importantly, men of "good sense and integrity"[31] such that sometimes local officials are permitted certain liberties that strain the general law because of what might be the requirements of their own particular situations.

It is also true, however, that such men in such offices will not be enough, because the justices of the peace do not themselves initiate action against administrative officers. The initiation of suits against officers of dereliction of duty cannot be put into the hands of the justices themselves for fear of concentrating in their hands an authority too great to be checked. This would be an imprudent mix of the executive and the judicial powers. It must be left, then, either to private individuals or a specially appointed public prosecutor to bring suit. America has chosen the former option, but this system is defective. The laws can be violated, or at least not carried out with vigor, without harm to any one person sufficient to cause his action. And it would be a great evil, says Tocqueville, for the laws to fall into disuse through a tacit agreement among the localities.

On the other hand, Tocqueville does not recommend the option of appointing public prosecutors either. The consequences of that system for "policing the administration" are as severe as the other.

> The New Englanders have never appointed a public prosecutor attached to the Court of Sessions, and one must appreciate how difficult it would have been for them to do so. If they had merely appointed a public prosecutor in each county town without providing him with subordinates in the townships, how would he have known more about what was going on within county than the members of Court of Sessions themselves? If he had been given subordinates in each township, the most formidable of powers, that of judicial administration, would have been centralized in his hands.[32]

It seems as if there is no right answer to this question. If the general public were virtuous enough not to allow the laws to fall into disuse but to bring suit against administrators when they were derelict, the system America has chosen would be the best possible one but that degree of popular virtue is not evident in America. Americans do sue their township and county officers but only as they are prompted by self-interest, not public spirit,[33] and that may not always be sufficient.

It is curious that the problem with the American system of administration seems to be just the reverse of that which we saw as the generic problem in democracy. The specific danger in America, that the laws may fall into disuse, is the opposite of the danger of a monolithic consolidation of all governmental powers. In the context of a discussion devoted to explaining the danger of administrative centralization in democracy, Tocqueville reveals that America runs just the opposite risk. America has carried decentralization too far even for its own convenience let alone for it to serve as a model for European nations in this respect.[34] Tocqueville's discussion of administrative decentralization and provincial liberty in America shows us the importance of these things, but at the same time it should make us wary of any program of decentralization. In fact, where the democratic tendency towards centralization was, unlike America, more legitimate and strong, we must wonder whether *any* institutional arrangement could even be imagined that would preserve a useful degree of provincial liberty and at the same time not interfere with the expression of the egalitarian passion. Wherever it becomes a matter of checking or limiting the passion for equality, any arrangement will surely fail. What makes American institutions work is that the love of equality, though untrammeled, still operates in a semi-barbarous condition. What Tocqueville says in the three chapters that remain in Part I of Volume I tends to confirm the suspicion that the structuring of governmental and administrative institutions is only an incidental part of Tocqueville's "new political science."

In chapters 6 and 7 Tocqueville discusses the role of the courts, and more broadly the role of legal and judicial procedures in resisting the problem of legislative centralism in American democracy. He is especially interested in judicial review as a tool to restrain the legislatures of both the states and the national government. His explanation of the effectiveness of judicial review in America emphasizes the special status of the Constitution in American law.[35] On one hand, the Constitution is not ordinary legislation subject to alteration by the legislature; therefore it can overrule inferior acts of the legislature. This contrasts with the situation in England where the absence of a written constitution and the absolute final supremacy of parliament necessarily go together. On the other hand, though the American Constitution is held to be the work of the sovereign people and not the legislature, it is changeable according to a procedure that the Constitution itself stipulates. The changeability of the American Constitution contrasts with the situation in France which, in a somewhat stricter but less practical vein, assumes that the constitution itself could not be altered without calling into question the legitimacy of the regime. America represents a compromise between the assumptions controlling the status of the constitutions of England and France. America can entrust to a transpolitical, judicial authority the power to void acts of the legislature and Americans are willing to tolerate that arrangement despite its anti-popular implications because they know that they hold the ultimate option of overruling their trans-political tribunal through Constitutional amendment.

Tocqueville's analysis of American judicial review amounts to the argument that it succeeds in checking the dangers of popular sovereignty, legislative centralism, by making a concession to the principle of popular sovereignty. It is, therefore, an institution that could easily be abused if the concession were to become too great in practice, or if it came to be recognized as insufficient because the procedure for Constitutional amendment is too cumbersome. For that reason Tocqueville recognizes that judicial review depends on a general disposition among Americans that contributes to the successful use rather than the abuse of the power. This point is reinforced by what Tocqueville says about the way that judicial review operates against ordinary legislation.

> Now, as soon as a judge refuses to apply a law in a case, it loses at once part of its moral force. Those who are harmed by it are notified of a means of escaping its obligations; lawsuits multiply, and that law becomes ineffective. Then one of two things happens: either the people change the Constitution or the legislature repeals the law.[36]

Tocqueville seems not to have understood that, once a law is held repugnant to the Constitution, no formal repeal is necessary in order to maintain the integrity of the American legal system; the law is simply void. But his way of describing how judicial review works emphasizes the dependency of judicial review on the moral force of the community. Thus we see in this particular instance another example of the general point that American institutions are successful in regulating the democratic passion because of certain features of American life that are not, in turn, derivative from those institutions.

In the latter part of chapter 6 and in chapter 7 Tocqueville describes the judicial procedure by which executive officers are held to account. It is in connection with this subject that Tocqueville reveals most openly his judgment of the deficiencies of American government. His first point is that American judges are given the right to try inferior executive officers for criminal acts. This power is a necessary consequence of the role that the courts play in Amer-

ican political life in general—they protect individual rights from
any and all abridgement by whatever authority, or by other individuals. "To forbid [the courts from trying executive officers] would
be taking away a natural right."[37] Thus Tocqueville observes an
important distinction between America and France: America has
never developed a full fledged system of "administrative law." Nevertheless, the system of holding executive officers to account for criminal acts would not be sufficient even in America to ensure the
responsibility of such officers. As Tocqueville said when speaking
of local officials, it is often the case that an officer will fail to do
his duty without involving any violation of any particular individual's rights. As a result, some form of "political jurisdiction" is
necessary by which a political body can pronounce judgments against
inferior officers for dereliction of duty.

> But in most free countries where the majority can never influence
> the courts as an absolute prince can, it is sometimes necessary
> temporarily to put judicial power into the hands of the repre-
> sentatives of society themselves. It has been thought better to
> merge these powers for a moment rather than to violate the
> necessary principle of unity of government.[38]

Now when the legislature assumes the power of political jurisdiction, there are two options from which a choice must be made
regarding the extent of the power. The legislature must either be
given the power to impose criminal penalties for the crimes that
the officer may have committed in connection with his dereliction
of duty, or the legislature may be limited simply to removing the
officer from his office and leave the imposition of criminal penalties
to the courts upon a subsequent trial procedure. The Americans
have chosen the second option, and after discussing the reasons
that they may have done so Tocqueville asserts that they have chosen
the more dangerous option. Because there are no criminal penalties
imposed consequent to an impeachment trial, the likelihood of an
impeachment proceeding is greater than it would otherwise be.
The threat of impeachment is a weapon by which American legislatures may tend to reduce the executive branch of their respective
governments to a strict subordinancy, concentrating all power in
their own hands.

> In preventing political tribunals from pronouncing judicial pen-
> alties, the Americans seem to me to have provided against the

more terrible consequences of legislative tyranny rather than against that tyranny itself. Everything considered, I wonder whether political jurisdiction as understood in the United States is not the most formidable weapon ever put into the majority's hands.

Once the American republics begin to degenerate, I think one will easily see that this is so; it will be enough to notice whether the number of political judgments increase.[39]

Tocqueville recognizes once again that the resistance to legislative centralism in America is critically dependent on fortunate, and temporary, circumstances.

The most important barrier to legislative centralism in the states is the federal structure of American government. The states simply do not have the powers by which to act as nations; in particular, the states do not conduct their own foreign policy and cannot make war, but, "War is the most important of all the events which can mark the life of a nation."[40] Even though the Americans feel themselves to be far more powerfully attached to their states than to the nation, the powers that the state governments are charged to exercise are incomplete. The states' powers do not provide the opportunity for the exercise of the political passions of a nation. The fact that the national government monopolizes those great powers through which a people comes to involve itself in a common life is highly problematical. Why does not the nation emerge as the locus of those centralizing instincts that Tocqueville thinks are so dangerous at the state level? The fact is that even though the national government has exclusive power over foreign policy it has little occasion to use it. So long as the federal powers remain relatively dormant, the states rather than the nation will continue to command the strongest political attachments of American citizens; but that answer only begs the question. How bright can the prospects for the survival of the union be if in any contest between the powers of the nation and the states the loyalties of the people will support the states? Tocqueville's response to that question, baldly put, is that in all likelihood the union will not survive. It is worth emphasizing as an all too commonly overlooked point that Tocqueville's judgment of the great American experiment in federal government, by which the union is happy and free like a small nation and also strong like a great one, is that the experiment will ultimately fail.

Therefore, in making a conflict between the two sovereignties less probably, the lawgivers of America did not destroy the causes of conflict.

One might go further and even say that in case of conflict they could not assure the preponderance of federal power.

They give the Union money and soldiers, but the states retained the love and the prejudices of the peoples.[41]

It is only due to good luck that Americans have not actually experienced the disadvantages of their federal union, and that good luck cannot go on forever.

Generally speaking, then, it is war which most obviously and dangerously reveals the weakness of a government, and I have shown that the inherent defect of federal governments is to be very weak.

———————-

How, then, does it come about that the American Union, protected though it be by the comparative perfection of its laws, does not dissolve in the midst of a great war? The reason is that it has no great wars to fear.[42]

These quotations do not prove that Tocqueville confidently predicts that the American union *will* dissolve. He says that the forces tending towards dissolution are the most dangerous ones in America, and that they will either cause the union to break up or a reaction will set in that will transform the union into a more consolidated national government. As he states in the concluding chapter of Volume I, "I say that it tends to grow daily weaker and that it is only the sovereignty of the Union which is in danger. That is what one now sees. What will the final result of this tendency be . . . ? That is hidden in the future, and I cannot pretend to lift the veil."[43] But the essential point remains that the union is a tenuous and unstable attempt to bind several inferior communities together into one political entity without generating a truly national identity. Rather than being a means by which the centralizing spirit of democracy can be regulated, the tenuousness of the American union reveals that American democracy remains in a semi-barbarous diffusion of mind and spirit. At this point the only possible lesson that can be drawn from all this is a negative one; we see what cannot be imitated. But the examination of Tocqueville's description of the structure of the national government promises to reveal some interesting speculations.

In the chapter on the national government Tocqueville devotes by far his most extensive attention to the executive. To oversimplify only slightly, the focus of his attention in the state governments is the legislature whereas the focus of his attention in the national government is the presidency. The themes of bicameralism and legislative representation are mentioned only casually. The reason for this, I suggest, is that the powers that the national government is charged to exercise are primarily the powers of "making war and peace, concluding commercial treaties, levying armies and equipping fleets."[44] The national powers of primary importance are the executive powers.

The leading characteristic of the national executive according to Tocqueville's description is its comparative weakness. The standard of comparison that Tocqueville uses is the French king, who is a much more significant figure than an American president because the king has a share in the legislative power. Indeed, Tocqueville rather overstates the powerlessness of the American president in this regard.

> The king shares with the chambers the right of introducing a law.
>
> The President has no similar initiative.
>
> The king is represented in the chambers by a number of agents who explain his intentions, support his opinions, and make his maxims of government prevail.
>
> The President has no entry into Congress; his ministers also are excluded, and it is only by indirect means that he can insinuate his influence and advice into that great body.
>
> ————————
>
> Beside the legislature, the President is an inferior and dependent power.[45]

But if the President were as weak in relation to the legislature as Tocqueville describes him, there would be an obvious question about his ability to maintain the degree of independence that is necessary to sustain the checks and balances among the branches for which the Constitution is famous. Tocqueville's answer to that question is just what we should have come to expect; the opportunities that the President has to use the powers that he does have are practically non-existent and therefore he is not an object of sufficient jealousy that his independence is in danger. Tocqueville makes this point by observing that in certain respects the American President does have limited attributes of a genuine monarch. "The President of the United States possesses almost royal prerogatives which he has no occasion to use, and the rights of which he has been able to make use so far are very circumscribed; the laws allow him to be strong, but circumstances have made him weak."[46]

There are at least two observations to be drawn from Tocqueville's disconcerting account of the reasons for which the American President does not become the simple minion of the democratic legislature. First, it means that the American executive is not an effective source of resistance to legislative centralism. Second, Tocqueville rather clearly indicates that in a more normally situated democracy than America—e.g., in France—the weakness of the American executive would be intolerable. Of all the comparisons that Tocqueville draws between the political institutions of America and France, the only one that Tocqueville thinks favors France is the share in the legislative power that the French executive has.

Following the description of the power of the American President, Tocqueville turns to discuss the system of Presidential election. While he praises the electoral college system that the framers devised for organizing the election, Tocqueville does not have much good to say about the actual conduct of American Presidential elections. Tocqueville does not join those who interpret the hooplah and antagonistic campaign rhetoric as a sign of the essential health of the regime; rather he describes with forboding and alarm the turmoil that the nation puts itself through to select the President.

> Nevertheless, one may consider the time of the Presidential election as a moment of national crisis.
>
> Moveover, in the United States as elsewhere, parties feel the need to rally around one man in order more easily to make themselves understood by the crowd. Generally, therefore, they use the presidential candidate's name as a symbol in whom they personify their theories. Hence the parties have a great interest in winning the election, not so much in order to make their doctrines triumph by the president-elect's help, as to show, by his election, that their doctrines have gained a majority.
>
> As the election draws near, intrigues grow more active and agitation is more lively and wider spread. The citizens divide up

into several camps, each of which takes its name from its can-
didate. The whole nation gets into a feverish state, the election
is the daily theme of comment in the newspapers and private
conversation, the object of every action and the subject of every
thought, and the sole interest for the moment. It is true that as
soon as fortune has pronounced, the ardor is dissipated, everything calms down, and the river which momentarily overflowed
its banks falls back to its bed. But was it not astonishing that such
a storm could have arisen?[47]

Obviously, the forbodings that Tocqueville expresses in these
passages are not grounded in any specific feature of the American
constitutional order other than the fact of the election itself. He
mentions additional inconveniences that stem from the same cause.
For example, he mentions that the reeligibility of the President is
a defect in the constitution of the presidency; for, as a result of this
feature, the President can be expected to calculate every move he
makes so as to maximize his chances of reelection and thus lose
the freedom to resist the popular will. "Reeligible . . . , the President
of the United States is only a docile instrument in the hands of the
majority."[48] On the other hand Tocqueville mentions "powerful arguments" that could be used to support the principle of reeligibility;
specifically, that the prohibition of reelection might exclude from
public service the very one who by his experience and public confidence could rule best. Even if these "powerful arguments" are not
sufficient to carry the day, they do mention important considerations
that a nation could not, under some circumstances, afford to ignore.

The inconveniences assoicated with the election of the chief
executive are severe enough in America to be worrisome. They
would be far more so in a European nation where the executive
was a more significant object of public attention and where the
wisdom of his practical experience needed more to be relied on.
What then? Does the net result of Tocqueville's observations on the
executive amount to the suggestion that the chief executive *not be
elected*? Is Tocqueville making a subtle endorsement for hereditary
monarchy? Or is he suggesting at least that we minimize the inconvenience of election by electing the executive for a life tenure?
Tocqueville does acknowledge that hereditary monarchies have one
great advantage—that their private and familial interest is connected with that of the state in a way that cannot be the case for a
temporarily elected executive.[49] The suggestion that Tocqueville is

recommending a rather strongly executive form of government for European democracy is tempting.

By this interpretation, there is a strong similarity between Tocqueville's analysis of how the American Constitution works and what Montesquieu depicted as the strength of the British system of government in the famous eleventh chapter of *Esprit des Lois*. This, of course, is hardly surprising in the light of the acknowledged debt of framers of the American Constitution to Montesquieu; however I suggest that Tocqueville's appreciation of the character of Montesquieu's argument was perhaps keener than that of the American framers. Montesquieu describes the British system as being an outgrowth of the "medieval" system of monarchy—and he says of that medieval institution that it was representative of the great advance over classical republican political philosophy to the advantage of the modern world.[50] In essence, the medieval system consisted of one king whose only interest was to be able to draw upon the force of the kingdom as a whole to provide for the common defense. Beyond military concerns, the king left domestic affairs to be administered at the provincial level. In Montesquieu's analysis of the British scheme of checks and balances among the legislative, judicial and executive branches of government, later development can be seen as a way of providing for the continuation of the ability of the medieval monarch to act with the necessary degree of independence and for the specific ends that are naturally connected with his private and familial interest but under more modern conditions. Tocqueville reads the American Constitution as a version of the example of Montesquieu but one that is weaker with regard to the essential element, the constitution of the executive. The Americans can get away with this weaker version of a quasi-monarchical constitution only because of their fortunate circumstances. The practical lesson is, as Montesquieu has indicated, that the key to any successful federal system of government in which local liberties are to be preserved is that the central government be strongly executive in character.

In Tocqueville's anlaysis of American federal government, *the* danger to provincial liberties in democracy is legislative centralism. The solution to that problem is for the central government to be primarily an executive government. Can democracy, however, be expected to tolerate anything like a monarchical system of government? It *is* possible to imagine a situation where the executive would be a democratic champion and captain. In view of what Tocqueville says about the likelihood of a single-headed despotism in democracy, one might say that the compatibility of one person rule with democratic spirit is all too great, such that Tocqueville must exert himself against such despotism above all other possible outcomes of democratic politics. However, the same spirit that might potentially support the despotism of a single person in democracy could also sustain an executive who would preserve the provincial liberties that are necessary to school democratic citizens, if only Tocqueville can instruct him in the wisdom of doing so. It is only an accident that in America the executive is the object of democratic jealousy residing in the legislature such that he is threatened with becoming their minion. In general, wherever the legislature is strong compared to executive, it will be the vehicle of democratic jealousy that will ultimately win out. But the legislature need not be strong in that way for the democratic passion to have form of expression.

Once again then, is Tocqueville subtly recommending a hereditary executive, or one elected for life? Beyond showing that his analysis points towards a strongly executive government in a situation less fortuitous than the United States, no flat affirmative or negative answer to the question is possible. The idea surely would be out of the question in America; its republican traditions and mores render the idea of monarchy beyond the pale of what Americans consider good government. Other countries have special circumstances too, though, and some of these may be highly favorable to executive government.

The only general point that can be drawn from Tocqueville's discussion of the executive power in America is that Tocqueville saw the independence of the executive as central to preserving provincial liberty against the danger of legislative centralism. Although there are dangers in executive power, there are risks in any conceivable institutional arrangement by which to secure liberty in democracy, and the correct choice depends upon the fitness of a particular people for a given set of institutions. As an example of Tocqueville's own attempt to follow the implicit advice he gives in the *Democracy*, as well as the complexity and the situational character of that advice, it is interesting to consider his performance as a member of the "Committee for the Constitution" during the aftermath of the Revolution of 1848 in France, that he reports in his *Recollections*.

> Beaumont proposed that the President should not be reeligible;
> I supported him vigorously, and the proposal was carried. On

this occasion we both fell into a great mistake which will, I fear, lead to very sad results. We had always been greatly struck with the dangers threatening liberty and public morality at the hands of a re-eligible president, who in order to secure his reelection would infallibly employ beforehand the immense resources for constraint and corruption which our laws and customs allow to the head of the Executive Power. Our minds were not supple or prompt enough to turn in time to see that, as soon as it was decided that the citizens themselves should directly choose the President, the evil was irreparable, and that it would only be increasing it rashly to undertake to hinder the people in their choice. This vote, and the great influence I brought to bear upon it, is my most unpleasant memory of that period.[51]

Tocqueville illustrates by the example of his own experience that "the legislator" must acknowledge and accomodate himself to the peculiar circumstances of the nation if he is to have any effect towards civilizing the passions of democracy. Tocqueville has shown the desireability of having a strong and relatively independent executive in order for modern democracy to enjoy the necessary competence in dealing with matters of concern to the nation and at the same time not to fall victim to the tendency towards the destruction of provincial liberties under legislative centralism. The specific form under which this general aim can be approximated will always depend on specific conditions, including the attitudes, the virtues, and the vices of the people. To the extent that this reading of Tocqueville's argument might have any influence upon the formation of such popular dispositions, that influence would be to cause the distinction between executive government and popular republican government to appear less wide and less firm than it is now generally taken to be.

Tocqueville's description of the American institutions of government almost sums up as a description of what will *not* work elsewhere, and why. American national government is not competent to provide that degree of uniformity that is a matter of importance even in secondary affairs, nor is it competent to fight a war. Americans do not feel the need of these things and so they are spared. Since Americans do not feel their common life as a nation, the problem of a centralizing passion is less severe. This is not to say that the Americans are without civic virtue; but only that the Americans have come accidentally and without understanding upon conditions conducive to the practice of their civic virtue and the healthy expression of their pride. For nations less fortunate, the inculcation and practice of civic virtue will have to be the conscious result of political art. If provincial government is to have the vitality that is necessary for it to serve as the practical school for freedom in nations more civilized than America, then the democratic citizenry must find a manner of expressing their public spirit that is *directly supportive* of provincial liberty. Is such a thing possible? It is to answer this question that Tocqueville turns in Part II of the first volume of *Democracy in America* where he analyzes the moral capacities of the ruling element in democracy—the *demos* itself. The non-exportability of American political institutions analysed in Part I serves to point to the fundamentality of this next task.

Three

The Character of the Democratic Sovereign

Volume I, Part II
Chapters 1–9

In the previous chapter it was shown that a proper arrangement of political institutions is only a necessary but not a sufficient condition for the preservation of liberty in democracy. Whatever particular institutions may be workable in the varied situations under which democracy may exist, they will depend for their success upon an uplifting of democracy's spirit lest they be crushed under the pressure of that form of jealousy that works through legislative centralism. No institutional arrangements are themselves sufficient to provide for the moral improvement of democracy that is, in turn, the prerequisite for good institutions.[1] For that reason it is necessary that Tocqueville turn, in the second part of his first volume, to the description of democracy's own character, to reveal its limitations and potentialities for wise and good government.

Tocqueville's task in the second part of the first volume is one that requires considerable subtlety, because, although Tocqueville addresses himself principally to someone he calls "the legislator," he does so in the context of a public expression which needs to find favor or at least respectful toleration by a democratic audience. The democratic audience will not, however, read his book from the same perspective nor see as far as "the legislator," and Tocqueville writes with those limitations in mind. Tocqueville's writing is a political art, and like a legislator, he needs to take into account the peculiarities of his material. When he analyses the mind and heart of modern democracy, he bears in mind that most of his readers are precisely the ones he is describing. What he shows about the limitations of the democratic mind and heart are the limitations of his audience. Tocqueville does not assume his general readership to be any other than those whose limited understanding, prejudices and vices he analyses in modern democracy, and he must temper the presentation of that very analysis.

Tocqueville introduces Part II by saying that he intends to describe the "instincts and passions" of the sovereign power in democracy.[2] He goes on, in chapter 1, to remind us that in America the sovereign power is that of the people which rules directly and without obstacle.[3] Following these two statements, Tocqueville takes up a discussion of American political parties. That discussion yields two main points. First, he shows that American democracy *is* a partisan government. Tocqueville does not agree with the view that democracy is a set of formally neutral procedures by which rival partisan factions may compete in an arena for the favor of the majority. Rather, the rivalry among parties that does exist is a surface phenomenon; on the deeper level democracy represents the victory of one side of a great partisan rivalry between the many and the few rich, and the victorious party brooks no genuinely serious opposition. The second point in the discussion of American parties is the ironic one that American democracy does not recognize the way and the degree to which it *is* a partisan government. One might say that the procedural view of democracy as neutral to the outcome of partisan struggle within majoritarian procedures is itself the democratic view. Democracy wrongly believes itself to be open to the full variety of points of view about justice and sound policy only because it has so effectively silenced the most interesting alternative to its own view.

Tocqueville then develops his argument by noting that there are three different kinds of party opposition that one can observe in the study of various political constitutions. In the first place there are structures that, while they are called parties, are in fact more than parties; they are potentially distinct nations.[4] This situation exists where there is a permanent opposition of interest between the rival camps. Only where there exists a common interest can there be "parties" in the stricter sense that Tocqueville defines, and of these more properly called parties there are two different forms.[5] During the times of a nation's life when it is searching about for answers to questions of fundamental values and formative principles, there arise "great parties;" the nation will tend to divide into two such parties following a natural, two-fold division "as old as the world" between those who wish to "restrict popular power," and those who wish to "extend it indefinitely."[6] In America, the example of great party opposition is exemplified by the Federalists and the Republicans.[7] The interesting thing about the great parties in America is that the Federalists were able to rule for a time even though their membership did not constitute a majority and even though the principal men of the party were by inclination of their moral character resistant to popular power. The Federalists were generally the sort of men who consider themselves born to lead, and Tocqueville suggests that in that they did themselves justice. The difference in the quality and the strength of men's ambition seems to constitute the fundamental division between the great parties and Tocqueville's judgment is that under circumstances that clearly call for great deeds where one can win lasting honor in public service, powerul ambition tends to produce political virtues. It is a tribute to American democracy that during the time of national peril, the extraordinary ambition that directs only a few was channeled to serve the nation and the extraordinary virtues of those few were recognized and honored. Federalists represented a natural aristocracy during the period when the need for such an aristocracy was universally recognized.

In contrast to the Federalist-Republican party politics, the politics of America in 1830 was defined by "small parties."[8] The transition, Tocqueville says, "[had] been a great gain in happiness but not in morality." The behavior of these small parties was as unprincipled as their aim, so that, "the selfishness of their character [was] openly displayed in all their actions."[9] But Tocqueville then shows that despite the dissimilarity between the great parties and the small ones, there was not a complete disjunction between the two phenomena. While a petty kind of selfishness actually animated the small parties, potentially the deeper passions actuated by the great and ancient division in society was present in them.[10] Tocqueville's example of this is the debate over the bank. The bank had become an issue over which small parties divided not because the American public had drawn the practical implications that that institution would have for their own private interests. The practical implications of the bank for each person's own well being were too complex and obscure to stand as the reason for partisan support or opposition. Rather, "the bank [was] a great establishment with an independent existence; the people, who destroy or evaluate all authorities, could do nothing against it, and that was a surprise.

With all the rest of society in motion, the sight of that stable point jars, and the people want to see if they can shake it, like everything else."[11] The transient and personal interest the people took in the issue of the bank derived from the way that it reflected the great issue of direct popular control. On inspection, "aristocratic or democratic passions can easily be found at the bottom of all parties and . . . though they may slip out of sight there, they are, as it were, the nerve and soul of the matter."[12]

Tocqueville's purpose in the chapter on parties can be recognized by contrasting what he says to the famous argument that is made by James Madison in Federalist no. 10. Madison argues the desirability of glossing over the great factious division that exists in all political societies between the few and the many lest the American democratic republic be dominated by the majority faction. He argues that by extending the sphere of the regime through republican institutions there can be brought in a variety of different kinds of economic interest no one of which will constitute a majority in its own right. The ruling majorities will then have to be formed through necessarily shifting constellations of private interest, and the natural majority will be rendered diffuse and politically impotent.[13] Tocqueville, however, deliberately scratches the surface of the gloss that Madison painted, so as to reveal the essentially factious character of even the petty politics in American democracy. He suggests that the absence of an open struggle between the many and the few is not due to the diffusion of the natural majority, but derives from the fact that the natural majority has been wholly victorious. The real reason why great parties exist only potentially in America is that the part of those who would limit the power of the people has been suppressed: "beneath [the] apparent unanimity deep divisions and real opposition still lie hidden."[14]

The chapter on parties extends and intensifies Tocqueville's description of the instincts and passions of the democratic sovereign. Such a description depends at the outset on the observation that certain passions and instincts are distinctive of democracy; they do not represent the full range of human passions and instincts but rather a selection from that range that has no particular claim to primacy. Democracy is, no less than any other regime that might be criticized on these grounds, the rule of one faction over the other; the fact that those who are suppressed are a distinct minority does not mean that their claims are unworthy or that their suppression is just. Democracy is unaware of the factiousness of its own rule and the questionableness of its justice because it has so completely silenced the opposing claims of the few whose personal ambition is great. That observation is the first one that Tocqueville makes in his description of the passions and instincts of the democratic sovereign. Tocqueville does not intend the characterization of democracy as a factious government to be a call to resistance; but what does emerge is that it does not and probably cannot understand itself well enough to follow Tocqueville's analysis and profit from its lessons.

Following the discussion of parties Tocqueville takes up two themes that are strongly related in his mind: freedom of the press and freedom of association in democracy. In Volume II as well as in Volume I of *Democracy in America*, when Tocqueville discusses freedom of the press in democracy he does so in conjunction with freedom of association. His statements in each of the two volumes respecting these themes are similar, but their contexts are different. In Volume II he describes the effects of freedom of the press and association on the formation of the sentiments of Americans, and of democratic citizens in general. In Volume I Tocqueville uses freedom of the press and of association as examples of the way and the degree to which the instincts and passions of the democratic sovereign are compatible with freedom.

Tocqueville confesses that he is not one who holds that freedom of the press is a supremely good thing in and of itself.[15] But the intrinsic desireability of freedom of the press is scarcely an issue for Tocqueville because freedom of the press is a necessary implication of democracy. "When each man is given a right to rule society, clearly one must recognize his capacity to choose between the different opinions debated among his contemporaries and to appreciate the various facts which may guide his judgment. The sovereignty of the people and the freedom of the press are therefore two entirely correlative things."[16] Moreover, the necessity of democracy's implication extends not only to some limited degree of freedom of the press, but to an absolute freedom. There is no half-way measure regarding freedom of the press that can be effective. The very act of rendering formal and authorative judgment on whether a given article of information or opinion may be published already lifts the words into the public eye.[17] This problem could only be avoided by giving an absolute power to some agency to impose a rule of censorship on their own authority, not subject to review or public scrutiny. But such a solution to the problem is worse than the problem, for that would eliminate all freedom of speech and writing.[18] The instincts and passions of democracy favor unrestricted freedom of the press much more than Tocqueville's own instincts and passions favor it.

The unrestricted freedom of the press need not occasion much danger nor even inconvenience to democracy. In America, the press enjoys unrestricted freedom and yet is not revolutionary or dangerous. The movement of thought that the American press registers is more similar to the Brownian motion of particles of dust than it is to any powerful current. This fact derives from the decentralization of American politics and administration. The American press exhibits its own decentralization which contributes to the agitated sameness of writing and thinking. "Of course, with so many combatants, neither discipline nor unity of action is possible and so each fights under its own flag. . . . Therefore American papers cannot raise those powerful currents of opinion which sweep away or sweep over the most powerful dikes."[19] While Tocqueville views the freedom of the press as little better than a necessary evil in democracy, or at least as a necessary risk, American democracy provides the example whereby the risk can be minimized without involving a hopeless attempt to compromise the principle.

It is, however, an oversimplification to say that the press is weak and ineffectual because of its diffuseness in American democracy. Tocqueville corrects that oversimplification towards the end of his chapter on the press. Along with the almost infinite variety of opinions that are registered on particular issues, there is an identifiable bias in the American press when looked at generally. The American press is a tool of what might be called the democratic mentality, and that mentality has a bias that is dominating and unchallengeable.[20] We see that even when it is well decentralized so as to pose less danger of provoking revolutionary passions, the democratic press is still criticizable as enforcing a vulgar and slothful intellectual conventionalism together with an unreasoned inclination towards egalitarian distribution of property. Freedom of the press contributes to intellectual sloth precisely because it advertises so many diverse opinions around any given subject. The net impression received by the disinterested citizen is that all the opinions presented are roughly equal in value; therefore there is no particular reason to abandon one's own opinion even if the reasons in its favor are none too clear even to oneself. Freedom of the press in democracy gives expression to what becomes a nearly universal, but bland and unphilosophical, skepticism. "In such ages people are not so ready to die for their opinions, but they do not change them; and there are to be found both fewer martyrs and fewer apostates."[21]

The bland skepticism to which freedom of the press contributes in democracy, while largely vacuous, is not without effect upon public policy. Democratic citizens may be skeptical of all opinions about what is good and bad for society in general, but they feel rather secure—all too secure—in their own estimate of what is good for themselves. Tocqueville's point is simply that habitual skeptics tend to reduce questions of social policy to the level of whose ox is gored. "When opinions are in doubt, men end by clinging only to instincts and material interests."[22] While the principle of the freedom of the press permits anyone to argue in print that society may have more to gain than it has to lose by preserving the freedom for individuals to pursue and to direct disproportionate wealth, the general, practical effect of that same freedom of the press tends to weaken the position of the wealthy. Democratic free press rather tunes the ear to hear the case for soaking the rich.

It may sharpen our focus on Tocqueville's purpose in discussing the freedom of the press to draw out that discussion and see how it bears on the contemporary debate over freedom of the press, and "free speech" in general. The current debate pits defenders of an absolute right to freedom of expression against those who argue that freedom of expression, like all freedoms, is subject to abuse and society must somehow bear the burden of distinguishing the use from the abuse. One of the most powerful and tireless spokesmen for the position that freedom of expression should be limited is Walter Berns, in his books *Freedom, Virtue and the First Amendment*, and *The First Amendment and the Future of American Democracy*.[23] Berns' argument is twofold. First, genuine freedom of expression is a more delicate and precarious value than his opponents realize. It has conditions: not only the physical security of the speaker or writer and his audience, but also psychological and moral conditions such as the freedom to take the podium without fear of character assassination and even the freedom to appeal to the more refined sensitivities and faculties of an audience without being drowned out or hooted out by an unfriendly "expression" of animal spirits. All these conditions can be violated by various kinds of inflammatory expressions, and in those cases, the expression deserves to be regulated or prohibited. The second consideration that Berns encourages is perhaps only a special case of the first. Perfect and absolute protection of all expression implies a fundamental neutrality toward the outcome of the contest among ideas, and therefore it implies that from the point of view of the regime all opinions are equal, and no one is or can be true. But to the extent that the perspective of the regime tends to become the perspective of the citizen, such a defense of freedom of expression robs intellectual activity and the contest among ideas of the ultimate and only real prize, namely knowledge of the truth. Under this situation, freedom of speech becomes a farcical thing; each citizen exercises his sacred right only to mouth a hymn of praise to a principle that has lost its content and its value. One is free to say whatever he chooses, and is even encouraged to express his own uniqueness and idiosyncracy as boldly as his imagination permits, but always with the proviso that it is only his own personal view and it carries no commanding significance. Meanwhile the proviso wins the day.[24]

Berns interestingly accords Tocqueville a gesture of deference in his book *The First Amendment and the Future of American Democracy*.[25] He observes that Tocqueville's defense of freedom of the press, while it is a defense of unrestricted freedom, does not derive from Tocqueville's own neutrality regarding which ideas are received and then form democratic society. Tocqueville is not a free speech liberal. But it is appropriate to remark that Tocqueville's position is not the same as Berns' either. Tocqueville's and Berns' observations on the consequences of freedom of expression are very nearly the same, but Tocqueville does not conclude with the desirability of limiting freedom of expression but rather settles for the position that the attempt is unpromising. While Tocqueville's observations are similar to Berns', his perspective and his purpose are different. Tocqueville is interested in preserving active involvement of democratic citizens in self-government and in fending off despotism, whereas Berns is concerned more directly with genuine intellectual freedom to pursue the truth, recognizing its own intrinsic value. Tocqueville's endorsement of freedom of the press in democracy, together with his full recognition of the effect of that freedom on the democratic mentality, shows that the disjunction between what Tocqueville hopes for by way of democratic freedom and the freedom of the mind from ignorance and false opinions. For Tocqueville, the truth is not what sets men free. All this accords with what Tocqueville said in his seminal chapter on Puritan New England. Men are able to attain political freedom on the level of untruth; the more genuine freedom of the mind is perhaps too distant a goal to be the standard of political life.

Tocqueville explicitly compares freedom of association in American democracy with freedom of the press, so that what he says in the chapter on freedom of association is presented as a sequel to the chapter immediately preceding it. It is unsurprising that Tocqueville endorses freedom of association; the advantages are extensions of what American democracy gains from the political and administrative decentralization that was described in Part I. "Apart from permanent associations such as townships, cities, and counties created by law, there are a quantity of others whose existence and growth are solely due to the initiative of individuals."[26] In this connection, freedom of association emerges as much more valuable than freedom of the press. Indeed, true freedom of association is probably the principle feature of a well-ordered democracy. "In our own day freedom of association has become a necessary guarantee against the tyranny of the majority . . . In countries where such associations do not exist, if private people did not artificially and temporarily create something like them, I see no other dike to hold back tyranny of whatever sort, and a great nation might with impunity be oppressed by some tiny faction or by a single man."[27]

Freedom of association is not only more important than freedom of the press in democracy, it is also more problematical. Tocqueville says that no nation can ever grant the same unlimited freedom to its citizens to associate for any purpose whatsoever as can be granted to write and print. "But *unlimited* freedom of association must not be entirely identified with freedom to write . . . A nation may set limits there without ceasing to be its own master; indeed, in order to remain its own master, it is sometimes necessary to do so."[28] The reason for the distinction does not turn on any attempt to draw a clear line between "speech" and "action;" rather it is that a state cannot wisely grant citizens liberty to associate for essentially conspiratorial purposes, whereas that problem simply does not exist when we are considering the freedom to *publish*. All examples of the use of freedom of the press are attempts to appeal to the authority of the majority, but some instances of freedom of association may involve attempts to displace the authority of the majority by another, and the democratic sovereign cannot be expected to tolerate such attempts.

The example of American democracy seems at first to belie the precept of caution regarding freedom of association that Tocqueville states. Americans do not set any limits on freedom of association—even for political purposes.[29] The result is in a way similar to the result that occurs in the case of the freedom of the press in America; since Americans have the freedom to associate for whatever reason they choose, they are not *driven* underground. The habit of thinking that forming an association is a perfectly legitimate enterprise causes the very idea of conspiracy to seem strange and unpleasant. "There are factions in America, but no conspirators ... Political associations in the United States are therefore peaceful in their objects and legal in the means used; and when they say that they only wish to prevail legally, in general they are telling the truth."[30] As in the case of freedom of the press, American democracy shows how freedom of association can be rendered less perilous by extending it and cultivating it.

The practically unlimited freedom of association is not abused in America due to the accidental circumstances that have been revealed before, and therefore America should not be limited in this respect. "In a country like the United States, where differences of opinion are only matters of nuance, the right of association can remain, so to say, without limits."[31] It does not occur to Americans to enter conspiracies, but this is only partly due to the freedom to associate; it also derives from the fact that in America potential differences over questions of public policy are not taken as seriously as they would be in Europe. Even this is only generally true. Sometimes even in America political passions focus on a broad and significant question, and when that happens the problem of regulating associations comes to fore. The example here is the convention that was privately initiated to oppose the tariff in 1831. Tocqueville praises the Americans for their skill in using the freedom of association in this case. He observes that, "The discussions were public, and from the very first day it took on an altogether legislative character."[32] But even given the facility with which the Americans used the freedom of association in this case to affect policy by legitimate means, the concomitant danger could not altogether be avoided. "Probably the convention of 1831 did greatly influence the attitude of the malcontents and prepared them for the open revolt of 1832 against the commercial laws of the Union."[33]

Freedom of association is critical to a well-ordered democracy. It operates as a substitute for and a bulwark against central power.

There is a danger, though, that the exercise of this freedom will lead to the formation of various sorts of partial societies harmful to the public good. To some extent, democracy can solve this problem almost automatically, in the same way it solves the problem of irresponsibility in the press. By permitting a wide diversity of associations as it permits a wide open freedom to publish, democracy enjoys the advantage that no one of them will have so great an effect on the public conscience to pose a severe threat. Still, complete freedom can almost never be wisely tolerated in the case of the freedom of association as it can in the case of the freedom of the press. Some prudent limits must be drawn and enforced. It remains to be seen how democracy can be expected to observe those limits.

In chapters 6 and 7 Tocqueville presents a broad and what appears to be a summary account of the advantages and the disadvantages of democracy. Despite the fact that Tocqueville says that he is "treading on live cinders"[34] in saying things that would be offensive either to the partisans of democracy or to its opponents, there is nothing in these chapters that is surprising on the basis of what Tocqueville has already said. Both the pros and the cons that Tocqueville records might vex the friends or enemies of democracy, but all the pros and cons have an obviousness such that those who do not accept them must still admit that here is where the argument is to be joined. The most serious disadvantages of democracy are its lack of regularity and stability both in the realm of lawmaking as well as administration, and also the birth of statesmanlike character among those in authority.[35] The legislation of democracy is so changeable because the democratic majority is and feels itself to be in direct control of the legislative process. Democracy passes laws in the same spirit that an absolute monarch issues decrees—with a view to changing them or rescinding them when conditions or wishes change. This same absoluteness of the dominion of the democratic majority leads to instability in the administration of the law. Just because democracy holds its civil service to be in a position of perfect subjection to the will of the majority in law, it has supreme confidence that it has nothing to fear from the exercise of administrative discretion, and therefore administrative discretion is used widely. for the same reason that a slave might be granted more privileges as his master gains confidence in his obedience, so "magistrates become freer as voting rights are wider spread and the duration of office shortened."[36]

As for the character of the men that democracy elects to lead, Tocqueville says that, "I take it as proved that those who consider universal suffrage as a guarantee of the excellence of the resulting choice suffer under a complete delusion. Universal suffrage has other advantages, but not that one."[37] Tocqueville cannot believe that the extremely difficult business of testing a person's mind or disposition can be accomplished by the majority of men on the basis of the exposure in a political campaign. Tocqueville goes so far as to approve the observation of Chancellor Kent that the persons most fit for office would probably not even step forth for they would instinctively recoil from a contest where their own virtues would be outshown by the low talents of popular appeal.

The most serious effect of the mutability of measures to which democracy is subject is in the realm of foreign policy. One might think of George F. Kennan's famous description of democratic foreign policy as similar to the behavior of a dinosaur—long periods of sleepy insensitivity to subtle changes in its environment interrupted by paroxysms of violence when the stimuli become too great. "Democracy seems to me much better suited to directing a peaceful society, or if necessary, to making some sudden and violent effort rather than to braying over a long period the great storms that beset a nation's political existence."[38] Tocqueville's unflinching account of the ineptitude of democracy in the realm of foreign policy and war should give his reader pause. Are those not damning indictments? It is true that the disadvantages of democracy are set off against advantages that he describes in the next chapter, and that over the long haul those advantages will render democracy more secure even against foreign dangers, but in the meantime, can democracy survive the pressures without collapsing into despotism? In view of the fact that Tocqueville thinks that it will require about a century before the advantages of democracy increase the real strength of society so that it will not be threatened with conquest by neighboring despotic states,[39] it almost seems that we are being led to despair. At least with regard to the prospects for Europe, how can it be expected that any fledgling democracy will be granted a century of peace and security? The severity of this conclusion indicates that this is not Tocqueville's final statement. As the book continues, the need for democracy to be made receptive to effective leadership from men of high character to guide it through its perils must be borne in mind.

The next chapter, on the real advantages of democratic government, is placed so as to make for a direct comparison with democracy's disadvantages. By citing the disadvantages first, and then the advantages, Tocqueville tends to understate the seriousness of disadvantages and also the necessity for correcting them. On the positive side he says that even though democracy is subject to a distressing mutability in its legislation, it is also important to bear in mind the spirit and general aim of legislation, and on this score democracy rates a plus. "One can therefore say . . . that democracy's aim in its legislation is more beneficial to humanity than that of aristocracy in its lawmaking."[40] The point here is carefully qualified; in connection with what was revealed in the chapter on parties it should be noted that Tocqueville explicitly says the general aim and interest of democratic legislation is not similar to that of *all* the governed.[41] Probably in no actual regime has such an ideal ever been realized. But the particular interest that the democratic sovereign serves, or seeks to serve, is at least similar to the interests of the majority of the citizens.

The more important advantages of democratic government are to be seen in connection with the form of public spirit that democratic citizens may exhibit. Since most men have the feeling that government reflects their own interests, an enlightened and rational patriotism develops.[42] Men respect each other's rights because they feel the advantage of the respect shown to their own. They respect the law because they think of its as their own work performed to their own ends. I stress that Tocqueville is not arguing here that citizens of democracy will be attached to their country and to the laws *because* they see them as useful to the pursuit of their own self-interest. Tocqueville maintains consistently that he has "no confidence in that calculated patriotism which is founded on interest and which a change of interests may destroy."[43] The enlightened patriotism of citizens of a democratic republic is a genuinely public emotion, but it is connected in the imagination with each man's self-interest and so it can be felt in the little day to day affairs of ordinary men. Having brought out the enduring quality of patriotism that can be expected of the citizens of a well-ordered republic, Tocqueville draws himself up and delivers his sweeping statement of the advantages and disadvantages of democracy in comparison with aristocracy.

What do you expect from society and its government? We must be clear about that.

Do you wish to raise mankind to an elevated and generous view of the things of this world? Do you want to inspire men with a certain scorn of material goods? Do you hope to engender deep convictions and prepare the way for acts of profound devotion? Are you concerned with refining mores, elevating manners, and causing the arts to blossom? Do you desire poetry, renown, and glory?

Do you set out to organize a nation so that it will have a powerful influence over all others? Do you expect it to attempt great enterprises and, whatever be the result of its efforts, to leave a great mark on history?

If in your view that should be the main object of men in society, do not support democratic government; it surely will not lead you to that goal.

But if you think it profitable to turn man's intellectual and moral activity toward the necessities of physical life and use them to produce well being, if you think that reason is more use to men than genius, if your object is not to create heroic virtues but rather tranquil habits, if you would rather contemplate vices than crimes and prefer fewer transgressions at the cost of fewer splendid deeds, if in place of a brilliant society you are content to live in one that is prosperous, and finally, if in your view the main object of government is not to achieve the greatest strength or glory for the nation as a whole, but to provide for every individual therein the utmost well-being, protecting him as far as possible from all afflictions, then it is good to make conditions equal and to establish a democratic government.[44]

There is a certain magnificence in these words. Tocqueville describes the aristocratic order without rancor, even with sensitivity and touching sympathy for the glorious pleasures that some men at least felt in those days. Then, with a dutiful resistance to whatever sadness one feels upon the death of anything grand, he turns his eyes towards the new dawn and finds that it too is beautiful. The atmosphere is cooler, the fiery colors are gone, but the light seems brighter. The passage has a charm like that of being drawn from physical excitement to a more intellectual pleasure. As much as is possible by the effect of written words, we begin to feel the calm and rational patriotism that Tocqueville has told us is the great advantage of democracy. Might one not almost wish for the book to end upon this note?

A wholly disenchanted reader of the conclusion of the chapter on democracy's advantages will be mindful that the advantages cited here are ones that democracy may exhibit, not ones that necessarily will be exhibited. In the light of what was said about democracy's disadvantages regarding the prospects for leadership and the conduct of foreign policy and war in the chapter before, it is doubtful whether democracy will ordinarily have the time or safety for it to develop its potential advantages. The picture of democracy as an enlightened society wherein every individual enjoys "the utmost well being," is a dream; not an impossible dream, but one we scarcely know how to approach given the perils of the world in which democratic society must develop.

In the discussion that follows, Tocqueville gives a different cast to his account of democracy. He writes, for the first time thematically and systematically, of the "omnipotence of the majority," and the "tyranny of the majority" in the United States. Following the presentation of the advantages of democratic society, Tocqueville reveals like a dash of cold water that in the United States the power of the majority is so completely untrammeled that it amounts to a tyrannical form of rule. The omnipotence of the majority sours the advantages and deepens the disadvantages of democracy that Tocqueville described in the two preceding chapters. The majority in the United States is so supremely powerful and confident of its power that not only does it make and unmake laws frankly for its own interest and on its own whim, but moreover it feels itself free to play fast and loose with its own laws. Tocqueville notes, to his shock, the recklessness Americans in Pennsylvania display towards their own electoral laws when they forcibly prevent Negroes from voting. Quoting himself in conversation with a citizen of Pennsylvania, he exclaims, "'What! The majority, privileged to make the law, wishes also to have the privilege of disobeying the law?'"[45]

The disturbing question that comes up in connection with Tocqueville's discussion in chapters 7 and 8 of Part II is whether it is possible for a democracy to be anything but a tyrannical government. Technically it is possible; Tocqueville says, "suppose you were to have a legislative body so composed that it represented the majority without being necessarily the slave of its passions, an executive power having a strength of its own, and a judicial power independent of the other two authorities; then you would still have a democratic government, but there would hardly be any remaining risk of tyranny."[46] Granted, if one could construct a government of checks and balances that would generate forces that might resist the expression of the majority, the tyranny of the majority would be avoided, but is that possible in fact? American government is famous for its system of checks and balances, and yet it is precisely in America that Tocqueville notes that there is no real check on the power of the majority.

> What I find most repulsive in America is not the extreme freedom reigning there but the shortage of guarantees against tyranny.
>
> When a man or a party suffers an injustice in the United States, to whom can he turn? To public opinion? That is what forms the majority. To the legislative body? It represents the majority and obeys it blindly. To the executive power? It is appointed by the majority and serves as its passive instrument. To the police? They are nothing but the majority under arms. A jury? A jury is the majority vested with the right to pronounce judgment; even the judges in certain states are elected by the majority.[47]

If the checks and balances of the American regime do not resolve the problem of majority tyranny because each element of the scheme represents the majority, then in principle the solution would be for a regime to be constructed of truly composite elements; one thinks of an "upper house" that represents an identifiable minority that would stand as a genuine bulwark against the majority will. But that solution is rejected by Tocqueville out of hand. As if to remind his reader that the problem of majority tyranny must be addressed from within the limits of a wholly democratic government, Tocqueville says plainly, "I have always considered what is called a mixed government to be a chimera. There is in truth no such thing as a mixed government (in the sense usually given to the words), since in any society one finds in the end some principle of action that dominates all the others."[48] In democracy that principle is the rule of the majority, and however we view it, it seems that we cannot escape its tyrannical implications.

In order to proceed against this seemingly hopeless difficulty, Tocqueville must refine his terms. Towards the conclusion of chapter 7, he draws a distinction between "arbitrary power and tyranny" that will be important for the remainder.

> Tyranny can use even the law as its instrument, and then it is no longer arbitrary; arbitrary power may be used in the interests of the ruled, and then it is not tyrannical.
>
> Tyranny ordinarily makes use of arbitrariness, but it can at need do without it.[49]

In the United States there is reason to fear both dangers; what was shown in chapter 5 on the disadvantages of democracy is repeated here. "In the United States that omnipotence of the majority which favors the legal despotism of the legislator also smiles on the arbitrary power of the magistrate."[50] Strictly speaking, the tyranny of the majority in democracy is indeed incontrovertible. It is only the arbitrariness to which democratic rule is prone that Tocqueville thinks can be mitigated.

In the chapter that follows, Tocqueville explains "What Tempers the Tyranny of the Majority in the United States."[51] He describes three institutions: administrative decentralization, the legal profession, and juries. Each of these three institutions succeeds in *tempering* the tyranny of the majority, in rendering it less prone to arbitrariness, precisely because it is compatible with the tyranny of the majority. Having already discussed administrative decentralization in detail in Part I, Tocqueville gives it only a passing reference at this point, but his argument is easier to see in connection with the description of the legal profession and the jury system. When he describes the jury system in America, Tocqueville does not forget what he has said earlier, that the jury is nothing but "the majority vested with the right to pronounce judgment," and therefore that it provides no guarantee that one's rights will not be abridged by the majority itself acting through the jury in accord with its own desire. But the jury is of some value in so far as it tends to "instill some of the habits of the judicial mind into every citizen."[52] By means of the jury system the democratic tyrant may be expected to come to pay a greater obeisance to the form of law.

The account of the role of the legal profession in American democracy goes to the same point. There is a certain affinity between the authority of the legal profession and the rule of the majority that makes it plausible that lawyers can become a principal medium through which the majority may express its will. This point in Tocqueville's argument is worth drawing out in particular because of its relevance to contemporary issues. Tocqueville says that lawyers are in general not of the same spirit as the democratic sovereign.[53] Lawyers tend to be conservative; their profession is one of knowing and conserving traditional forms. The Federalist party that Tocqueville described earlier was imbued with the spirit natural to lawyers. In a sense, it is possible to describe the lawyers as an aristocracy. Nevertheless there is a profound kinship between the habit of legal reasoning and the mentality that characterizes the democratic majority. Indeed, in an appendix to *Democracy in America* Tocqueville even suggests that the movement towards democratic equality in western history may well have begun when lawyers first became significant in government.[54] The kinship between democracy and lawyering lies in the fact that the very idea of law is that a number of different individuals can be comprehended within the terms of a single generality. The law, as we say, is "no respecter of persons," it treats unequals as if they were equals for whatever specific purpose the law has. Democracy's habit of mind is to push the idea behind the rule of law as far as imagination and power permit; it is impatient and suspicious of any claim of special circumstance or interest that requires an exception to the general rule. Tocqueville's famous aphorism, "There is hardly a political question in the United States which does not sooner or later turn into a judicial one,"[55] is an indication of this natural kinship between democracy and the kind of reasoning that lawyers and judges do. In a word, democracy tends to make the necessary presumption of any legal system—equality before the law—into the object of its overall social policy. All this is not to gainsay that democracy *may* lead to the enhancement of arbitrary power when such power is believed to be exercised in the service of the majority's wishes, but it does explain why lawyers can have an extraordinary influence in democratic government despite their conservatism and even their spiritual connection with aristocracy. The legal profession can have some tempering effect on the tyranny of the majority only in so far as it supports the absolute right of the majority to rule for whatever interest it may conceive.

Chapter 9 of Part II, entitled "The Main Causes Tending to Maintain a Democratic Republic in the United States,"[56] should be read as the concluding chapter among those that form the main line of argument in Part II of Volume I because Tocqueville says that the one chapter that still remains, on the condition of the three races that occupy the United States, is tangential to his proper subject. The discussion in chapter 9 is an extention of chapter 8, but it is considerably broader in its scope. Whereas chapter 8 delineated three institutions through which the tyrannical majority might be made to comport with legal forms, we did not learn what *resists* the majority's inclination to arbitrary rule. Administrative decentralization, the legal profession, and the jury system are devices that are compatible with democracy and they are ones through which the democratic majority learns to use the law. But none of these institutions are capable of resisting the majority if it wished to act arbitrarily, nor do they, in and of themselves, sufficiently account for the fact that the American majority does not conceive such wishes. The status of the argument at this point is practically the same as it was at the end of Part I, only the institutions of the legal profession and the jury system have been added to administrative decentralization. It remains the case that these institutions depend upon something external to themselves so that they will be preserved from the destructive effects of the most arbitrary and vicious form of the love of equality. The institutions discussed in chapter 8 can be useful only if democracy has the mind and spirit to use them; chapter 9 contains the promise that the fundamental influences upon democracy's mind and spirit will be explained.

There are three main causes that tend to maintain a democratic republic in the United States: the physical circumstances of the continent, the laws, and the mores of the people.[57] The information that Tocqueville presents regarding the first two sets of causes is not new; he only reiterates what has been presented before in order to establish the comparative importance among the three kinds of causes. His intent is to show that the physical conditions of American democracy are the least important reason for the survival of the democratic republic, the laws are next in order of importance, and mores are the most important.[58]

The physical circumstances in America support the democratic republic because they discourage the formation and expression of collective emotions that might pose a threat to the vitality of America's free institutions.[59] Americans do not have the opportunity to act together as a nation towards one single aim, the outstanding example of which is victory in war, and on the other hand they do have the almost boundless opportunity to pursue private gain without coming into direct conflict with each other. The energies of the Americans are nearly consumed in private pursuits; they do not conceive such great public enterprises in the name of which legal procedures and provincial liberties might have to yield. The American laws and political institutions depend critically on the way that American physical circumstances preserve them from the collective emotions of the majority. Nevertheless, Tocqueville insists that laws are in general more important than physical conditions, and mores are even still more important. He reasons that there are other nations in the new world as well favored by fortune as the United States, but they have not succeeded in founding or preserving a democratic republic, whereas mores "can turn even the most un-favorable circumstances and worst laws to advantage."[60] The con-clusion to be drawn from the statement of the relative importance of the three sets of causes is that although mores are the most important factor in explaining the success of the laws, the mores must be just those which are able to make use of the physical circumstances in the right way. What Tocqueville says about the relative importance of the different causes that maintain a demo-cratic republic in the United States can be grasped by drawing a parallel to some productive art. Which, for instance, is most im-portant for a house to be built: the presence of timbers and nails, or the knowledge of what to do with them? Tocqueville's answer is that both are necessary if one particular blueprint is to be followed, but in a more general sense, the man who knows what is required in a house can make use of a number of different kinds of mate-rials—stones and mud for example—in place of timber and nails. To carry the analogy one step further with reference to the Amer-ican situation, the materials of which the American republic was constructed practically fell into place without needing much inge-nuity from the builders.

Not even in America, though, can favorable physical circum-stances explain how a democratic republic is preserved. The mores of the Americans had to be right lest they misuse their blessings. Broadly considered, the central purpose of Part II of Volume I has been to bring to light this fact. In Part I we learned how the laws and political institutions in America depended on the fortuitous circumstances of the American continent; the effect of Part II has been to shift our attention from physical conditions to mores as the ultimate reason for America's success. So long as we focus on Amer-ica's physical conditions, we are looking only to a negative argu-ment—we see how American institutions are preserved against the vicious form of the love of equality because men are busy with private affairs. But the analysis in Part II of the "instincts and passions" of that collective entity, the democratic sovereign, shows how incomplete is the account of American democracy that holds its citizens animated exclusively or even principally by private pas-sions. It must be the case that the "instincts and passions" of the American democratic sovereign have taken a virtuous form, one that allows individuals the pursuit of private gain because it is generally seen as socially beneficial. The longest section of chapter

9 is devoted to explicating the roots of the civic virtue, or mores, of the American democratic sovereign.

The discussion of the mores of the American majority is in substance a discussion of American religion. The value of religion in preserving a democratic republic is that it constrains imagination and tames ambition.

> The imagination of the Americans, therefore, even in its greatest aberrations, is circumspect and hesitant; it is embarrassed from the start and leaves its work unfinished. These habits of restraint are found again in political society and singularly favor the tranquility of the people as well as the durability of the institutions they have adopted.... American revolutionaries are obliged to profess a certain respect for Christian morality and equity, and that does not allow them easily to break the laws when those are opposed to the executions of their designs; nor would they find it easy to surmount the scruples of their partisans even if they were able to get over their own. Up till now no one in the United States has dared to profess the maxim that everything is allowed in the interests of society, an impious maxim apparently invented in an age of freedom in order to legitimize every future tyrant.[61]

Precisely because religion tends to restrain the ambition and imagination of the democratic majority, the question is how can it be effective. Has Tocqueville not repeatedly said that nothing that attempts to resist the force of the majority can survive for long in a democratic society? In order to answer this question it is necessary to discover some harmony between American democracy and American religion. Such a harmony must in fact exist in any regime where religion is strong and where political institutions are sustained rather than threatened by religion. Tocqueville informs us that, "Every religion has some political opinion linked to it by affinity. The spirit of man, left to its own bent, will regulate political society and the City of God in uniform fashion; it will, if I dare put it so, seek to *harmonize* earth with heaven."[62] How then can the moderating spirit of religion harmonize with the spirit of democracy?

Tocqueville indicates that there are two different examples of how religion is compatible with American democracy. The first example is American Catholicism. By one measure American Catholics are the most democratic as well as the most republican sect in the United States. However, the reasons that they are devoted to democracy and republicanism are not especially flattering. "In matters of dogma the Catholic faith places all intellects on the same level; the learned men and the ignorant, the genius and the common herd, must all subscribe to the same details of belief; . . . Catholicism may dispose the faithful to obedience, but it does not prepare them for inequality. However, I would say that Protestantism in general orients men much less towards equality than towards independence."[63] Although the Catholics are egalitarians, their propensities run in the same vein as the worst ones in democracy. They are accustomed to govern their behavior according to a general dogma that prescribes every detail, with no respect for the differences among individuals. The equality they imagine is the equality of absolute obedience rather than that of personal freedom and independence.

It is true that American Catholics are partisans of political freedom as well as democratic equality, but that disposition is due to the accident that they are in a minority and political freedom protects them from suppression by the majority. "The Catholics are in a minority, and it is important for them that all rights should be respected so that they can be sure to enjoy their own in freedom. [Thus] they are led, perhaps in spite of themselves, towards political doctrines which, maybe, they would adopt with less zeal were they rich and predominant."[64] The harmony between Catholicism and democratic equality is natural; the harmony between Catholicism and republican freedom is based on accident and calculation. It is therefore fortunate that the Catholics are not the dominant force.

The other example of religion in America is Protestantism. This example is both more promising and more complex. In speaking of the disposition of the Protestants, Tocqueville reveals that theirs is a highly worldly kind of faith. He says, "I do not know if all Americans have faith in their religion—for who can read the secrets of the heart? —but I am sure that they think it necessary to the maintenance of republican institutions. That is not the view of one class or party among the citizens, but of the whole nation; it is found in all ranks."[65] There is obviously something question-begging as well as disconcerting about this description of the way most Americans think about religion. We have been brought to think that in religion we might discover the ultimate grounds for the remarkable prudence of American democrats. Now it appears that religion itself is honored only by virtue of the fact that Americans have a prudent regard for its political value! The disappointing conclusion from this would be that religion is simply one more device that a prudent people use to maintain their liberty; we are no closer to knowing what the reasons are that this people exhibit prudence to such a remarkable degree. It is perhaps even more troublesome that this account of religion in American makes of it an *unnecessary* and *useless* device. For although it is often the case that people have the beliefs that are convenient for them to have, it is not true that calculation dictates to the conscience what it should feel. If the Americans are conscious of the fact that what they do is to pay lip service to the precepts of Christian morality because they are politically useful, it is hard to imagine how that same religion could effectively form the souls and restrain the imaginations of its practitioners. To the extent that Americans understand themselves to know the real reasons that support Christian morality, could they not as well dispense with the idea of divine support as excess baggage?

Such puzzles are based on a thin reading of what Tocqueville says about American religion, and religion in general. In truth, the religious faith of the Americans is genuine and strong, and it is fundamentally important to the explanation of their political prudence. In order to grasp fully the role that religion plays in the formation of American character and the preservation of political liberty it is necessary to look beyond the account of the importance of religion that the Americans themselves report. Americans think that religion is politically useful, but that the political bond is different from what ties men to religion as the calculation of what serves one's own interests differs from faith. That is how the Americans understand the separation of church and state. But the emotions and motives that lead men to honor their religious duties and their political ones cannot be so fundamentally separate. Recalling that "The spirit of man, left to his own bent, will...seek to harmonize earth with heaven," we need to look for a deeper connection between American religion and politics.

In order to pursue further the emotional motivational connection between religion and politics, Tocqueville needs to raise the question of the psychological necessity for faith. What needs of the human soul does it answer? He then tries to answer the question from a "purely from a human point of view, [from which it can be seen that] all religions derive an element of strength which will never fail from man himself, because it is attached to one of the constituent principles of human nature."

The short space of sixty years can never shut in the whole of
man's imagination; the incomplete joys of this world will never
satisfy his heart. Alone among all created beings, man shows a
natural disgust for existence and an immense longing to exist;
he scorns life and fears annihilation. These different instincts
constantly drive his soul towards contemplation of the next world,
and it is religion that leads him thither. Religion, therefore, is
only one particular form of hope, and it is as natural to the
human heart as hope itself. It is by a sort of intellectual aberation,
and in a way, by doing violence to their own nature, that men
detach themselves from religious beliefs; an invincible inclination
draws them back. Incredulity is an accident; faith is the only
permanent state of mankind.[66]

The need to hope that the significance of our lives is not exhausted during the time that we draw breath is productive of a
faith that that is so. Such faith is so natural among the majority of
mankind that it requires no political support, or any authorative
support whatsoever. All that is necessary for such faith to flower is
that it be preserved against things that would interfere with it.
Tocqueville says further that, in general, there are two things that
can interfere with men's natural faith: schism and indifference,[67]
and he explains how the effects of both can be avoided. Schism
among opposing sects is a problem only when the separation of
church and state is not properly observed. There is nothing in the
natural need for religion that makes dogmatic distinctness necessary, so there would be no issue were it not for the accident that
necessarily distinct political systems invest religion with distinct features that faith does not know how to compromise.

When a religion seeks to found its sway only on the longing for
immortality equally tormenting every human heart, it can aspire
to universality; but when it comes to uniting itself with a government, it must adopt maxims which apply only to certain nations. Therefore, by allying itself with any political power, religion
increases its strength over some but forfeits the hope of reigning
over all.[68]

America shows by way of example how the problem of religious
schism can be negated by separating political and religious authority.
Indifference, too, becomes a political problem only when there
exists an improper mix between politics and religion. This is not

to say that there is no indifference to religion among Americans, for despite the naturalness of religious faith there will always be some who deny themselves the satisfaction of faith and in the modern world such self-denial is not rare. Americans who deny faith in their own hearts, however, do not burden the conscience of their fellow citizens by preaching such denial. There is no reason for them to do so except where religion is made use of by political partisans such that to oppose their measures one must oppose their religion. In America that does not happen, and so the unbelievers can afford to be both kind and sensible in allowing those who profess faith to do so without embarrassment.

> One sees some men lose, as from forgetfulness, the object of their dearest hopes. Carried away by an imperceptible current against which they do not have the courage to struggle but to which they yield with regret, they abandon the faith they love to follow the doubt that leads them to despair ... In such ages beliefs are forsaken through indifference rather than from hate; without being rejected, they fall away. The unbeliever, no longer thinking religion true, still considers it useful. Paying attention to the human side of religious beliefs, he recognizes their sway over mores and their influence over laws. He understands their power to lead men to live in peace and gently to prepare them for death. Therefore he regrets his faith after losing it, and deprived of a blessing whose value he fully appreciates, he fears to take it away from those who still have it.[69]

That the strength of the faith that most Americans have lies in its doctrinal nonspecificity explains their toleration. Tocqueville does not accuse Americans of hypocrisy because their professed religious toleration is not productive of an actual variety among religious sects. On the contrary, he applauds the fact that toleration is itself a sort of article of faith, which is itself not very tolerant of opposition. The Americans have a sort of faith that can be called "natural," which holds that God loves an honest conscience rather than a specific understanding. Their disposition to tolerance bespeaks a trust in what one might call God's humanity. On this reflection we can understand the affinity between American Protestantism and democracy that Tocqueville said at the outset of the discussion of religion must exist. In a way quite consistent with the separation between church and state, the Americans have given their own expression to that "spirit of man [which seeks to] regulate political society and the City of God in uniform fashion."

It is instructive to compare what Tocqueville says of religion in democratic America with the conclusion of Rousseau's famous discussion of the civil religion in the fourth book of *The Social Contract*.[70] Rousseau argues there that it is absolutely necessary for political authority to be supported by religion if there is to exist a true general will, and he goes on to consider three candidates, so to speak, for the civil religion: the religion of pagan antiquity, orthodox Catholicism ("the religion of the priest"), and finally what he calls "the religion of man," which he identifies with the original teachings of the Gospels. Rousseau rejects each of these kinds of religion, and in so doing he seems to have left himself with no possible answer to the paramount need for civil religion! Rousseau then recommends, in what seems at first a lame last ditch effort, that the social contract be tolerant towards *any* religion, so long as it is itself tolerant of others. Only the doctrine that there is no salvation outside the church must be declared anathema.[71] The question that emerges from Rousseau's case for a civil religion is obvious: how can the toleration of many different religions answer the need for the social contract to be supported by religious faith? Rousseau seems to settle for mere neutrality rather than positive support in his final position. But on reflection, the neutrality between religion and politics that Rousseau recommends is an illusion. In fact Rousseau's point is the same as Tocqueville's, that religious toleration derives from what is itself an article of faith that God loves an honest conscience. The fact that there is still one doctrine that must be declared anathema is proof that the toleration of many different religions is not absolute. What seems at first to be the collapse of the attempt to find the particular religion that answers perfectly the needs of the social contract turns out to be the preparation for the emergence of that truly "civil religion" of the sacredness and sovereignty on the individual conscience. Rousseau is of the opinion, which Tocqueville shares fully, that faith is perfectly compatible with the citizens' devotion to their particular regime as well as supportive of the social contract as the source of the legitimate authority of the state.

The question remains, however, whether Tocqueville's account of religion is satisfactory. Tocqueville seems to say that the religion that men need is practically contentless. But, then, does it not beg a question? Just what moral or theological precepts does true "conscience" espouse? Alternatively, are there not examples of conflict between conscientious men, that would be irresolvable according to that standard alone? How then can the idea of the sanctity of the conscience nourish those who wish from their faith that it throw light upon their duty? From this reflection it would appear that, among those in the modern world who are left with doubt where there should be faith, are those who have thought through the toleration and humanity that the religion of modern democracy teaches and have found it utterly incapable of answering the deepest needs of their souls. As far as Tocqueville is concerned, there is simply no answer to such persons or such needs. He leaves the question with the remark that those who are able to bear religious doubt will not generally wish to deny the happiness that is possible for others or disturb the public tranquility by attacking modern faith. And as for his own happiness? Tocqueville's own happiness is regretfully nowhere a theme of *Democracy in America* nor any other example of his writing. The most flattering statement that can be made on this point is that Tocqueville puts his duty first, and lets his happiness take care of itself as best it can.

The first nine chapters of Part II, Volume I of *Democracy in America* make a rather long text, so I will briefly outline the structure of the argument present there before striking the final note. The purpose of Part II is to analyze the instincts and passions of the democratic sovereign—the majority; Tocqueville quite consciously assumes that this collectivity can be understood by treating it as if it were a natural individual. The government of democracy is indeed a partisan regime. It serves the distinctive interests of the democratic sovereign. The democratic sovereign is, however, practically unaware of the partisan character of its own rule; having forgotten the claims of its opponents it believes itself to be representative of every element of humanity. Because of the obliviousness of the democratic sovereign to the partisan character of its own rule, it believes that it can tolerate complete freedom of expression and of association with impunity. In the case of the freedom of expression this belief corresponds to the facts, although not quite in the way that the democratic sovereign thinks; but with regard to the more important freedom, of association, the weakness of democracy's understanding has to be corrected. Moving from these examples to a general inventory of the advantages and the disadvantages of democracy, it appears that the comparison favors democratic government over any conceivable alternative; but the disadvantages are serious and are the grounds for an important practical question. To the extent that the majority rule directly in democracy, the quality of leadership suffers, and in the fields of foreign policy especially, this disadvantage may be devastating. Can democracy's need for leadership in a world full of dangers be answered? Further analysis is needed.

Democracy is essentially a tyranny, according to the classical and still acceptable definition of the tyrant as he who rules in his own interest rather than for the sake of the common good. Tyranny, however, may not always be bad. Tyranny is especially bad when it leads to arbitrary government, as it has a tendency to do, but that tendency can be avoided without involving any direct opposition to the democratic tyrant. America displays institutions that are compatible with democratic government while they do resist the tendency towards arbitrariness. Through them, Americans learn to be law-abiding. But how do these institutions themselves stand up against the potential lawlessness of democratic rule? What is the basic reason for the self-control of American democratic citizens? The answer is that the laws, the physical conditions of the country, and the mores of the Americans all work together to account for the virtues of the Americans, but in general mores are the controlling factor. Religion is of central and comprehensive importance to the development of American mores, and on examination the religion of the preponderance of Americans is similar to the "civil religion" on which Rousseau wrote in *The Social Contract*, and it works in the same way. The civil religion of the Americans tames the pride and moral recklessness that could be summarized in the slogan that everything is permissible in the service of the public good. The democratic sovereign can be expected to honor established procedures and legal forms and resist the temptation to rule directly on each question at hand. Such a taming trust in the sufficiency of law makes American institutions less vulnerable to the whims of the democratic sovereign.

The more clearly we see the civil religion as the formative principle of the mores of the Americans that permit them to use their governmental institutions the more clearly do we see that those specific institutions need not be duplicated in other countries. That is fortunate, because it has been shown that American institutions would work nowhere else but in America. Tocqueville has very little to say about just what kind of institutions *would* work for European democracies; but the hints that he gives consistently indicate that European nations require a more executive government than America exhibits. Tocqueville cautiously ventures, without elaboration, near the end of chapter 9,

> Is it, then, impossible to imagine a government founded on the genuine will of the majority, but a majority which, repressing its natural instincts for equality for the sake of order and stability of the state, would consent to invest *one family or one man** with all the attributes of executive power? Can one not imagine a democratic society in which national strength would be more centralized than in the United States and in which the people exercised a less direct and less irresistable sway over public affairs, but yet where each citizen, invested with certain rights, would take part within his sphere in the proceedings of the government?"[72]

Part II ends with the speculation with which Part I ended. Like Machiavelli in his *Discoursi*, Tocqueville apparently thinks that there is less difference than is generally supposed between a republic and a principality. To put it in a Machiavellian formula, just as a wise prince needs to understand the degree of his dependence on the people, a well-ordered and wise people require a head.[73] "The legislator" who serves as Tocqueville's addressee in *Democracy in America* is not simply a construct drawn up so as to give the book literary focus. Some unknown young Frenchman, favored by fortune and extraordinary ambition, is invited to draw encouragement and practical lessons from this book beyond what the general reader is likely to find.

Four

The Naturalness
of Democracy

Volume I, Part II, Chapter 10

With the discussion of religion in American democracy in chapter 9, the second and final part of Volume I might end. The analysis of the problems of democracy and the structure of the measures that might solve those problems has been completed. Tocqueville adds one more chapter, however, because he says that his reader will probably be curious about a number of things that characterize America even though they are not features of democracy *per se* and he does not wish to disappoint that curiosity too much. Chapter 10, on "the Present State and Probable Future of the Three Races that inhabit the Territory of the United States," reviews subjects that are "like tangents to [his] subject being American, but not democratic, [while his] main business has been to describe democracy."[1]

While chapter 10 is strictly speaking tangential to the line of argument in Volume I, it is not unimportant. The additional curiosity that Tocqueville expects his readers will feel is appropriate. The fact that only in chapter 10 does Tocqueville extend his gaze beyond the horizon of the democratic order, and consider mankind in a three-fold variety of social conditions, indicates the importance of this chapter. The Reds, the Blacks, and the Whites seem to represent a comparison of three fundamentally alternative conditions: aristocratic but barbaric freedom, abject servitude, and democratic equality. In fact, the scope of chapter 10 is broader than the rest of the volume, for here Tocqueville goes beyond the recommendations for the improvement of democracy to illustrate the contest between democracy and competing forms of social order. The contest between the Reds and the Whites demonstrates what might be called the natural primacy of democratic equality over the pre-democratic order; and that same comparison is confirmed by Tocqueville's showing of the effects on civilization of the fundamental violation of democratic equality in Negro slavery.

The displacement of the Indians by the Whites in America seems to be a clear parallel to the displacement of the feudal civilization by what would finally emerge as modern democracy. The Indians appear like a caricature of the feudal nobles. They suffered from too high an opinion of themselves, and this very pride made them weak before the Whites. It is critical that they considered it beneath their station to work. War and hunting were the only pursuits their sense of honor permitted them.[2] When the advance of the White farmer drove away the Indian's game, the thought of their tilling the soil never entered their heads, and so they fled with the deer.[3] Were the Indians able to subsist on the wild fruits of the land, they might have successfully retained their proud refusal to labor even in the absence of game. But the deepest element of their tragedy is that the slightest touch of the White civilization filled the Indians with new wants that could not be satisfied by means familiar to them. Their attempt to satisfy their new hungers by exchanging the booty of the hunt with Whites put still greater strain on the game resources and deepened the scarcity.[4] Both the Indians' social structure and the psychic structure were pathetically weak and vulnerable. Beyond the pathos generated by Tocqueville's touching description, we cannot help but conclude that the Indian culture was, literally, not fit to survive.

The advance of the Whites at the expense of the Indians was by no means simply a savage conflict. The Whites removed the Indians with the greatest show of deference to humanity, and under the color of legal form. Moreover, the Indians did not defend themselves in the manner of brutes. Tocqueville reproduces the essence of both arguments, and, in so doing, he shows the weakness of both. As for the Indians, they make an argument in defense of their natural right to their property.

> 'From time immemorial, our common Father, who is in heaven, has given our ancestors the land we occupy; our ancestors have transmitted it to us as their heritage. We have preserved it with respect, for it contains their ashes. Have we ever ceded or lost this heritage? Permit us to ask you humbly what better right a

nation can have to a country than the right of inheritance and immemorial possession? We know that the state of Georgia and the President of the United States claim today that we have lost this right. But this seems to us a gratuitous allegation. At what time have we lost it? What crime have we committed which could deprive us of our homeland? . . . '

Such is the language of the Indians; what they say is true; what they foresee seems to me inevitable.[5]

The case of the Indians is eloquent and touching—and it contains the truth that justice is on the side of the Indians. But Tocqueville's obvious sympathetic feelings for the Indians does not determine his final judgment. To grasp Tocqueville's final judgment, it is necessary to consider the case that is made by the Whites.

See inter alia the report of February 24, 1830, written by Mr. Bell on behalf of the Committee on Indian Affairs, in which on page 5 it is established by very logical arguments and most learnedly proved that: 'The fundamental principle, that the Indians have no rights by virtue of their ancient possession either of soil or sovereignty, has never been abandoned either expressly or by implication.'

Reading this report, written, moreover, by an able man, one is astonished at the facility and ease with which, from the very first words, the author disposes of arguments founded on natural right and reason, which he calls abstract and theoretical principles. The more I think about it, the more I feel that the only difference between civilized and uncivilized man with regard to justice is this: the former contests the justice of rights, *the latter simply violates them.*[6] (my emphasis)

The astonishingly cavalier hypocrisy in the argument set forth by Mr. Bell should not obscure Tocqueville's concurrent admission that the Indians' argument is also, in its own way, hypocritical. The Whites assume an obligation to contest the justice of the Indians' claims—an obligation that they cannot possibly meet. But clearly, if the shoe were on the other foot, the Indians would feel no such compunction. The Whites feel obliged to contest the justice of the Indians' argument because the Whites are a property-holding civilization, and the very notion of property seems to presume a notion of natural right that must be honored even in the breach. But the Indians, Tocqueville says, own no property. He asserts that they

occupy the land but they do not own it.[7] It would seem, then, that
in their appeal to the Whites in behalf of the natural right to their
property they make a kind of argument that they have no occasion
to make except to the Whites, and even then they are forced to
make it only because they are the weaker party. This reflection
shows the problematical grounds of the argument employed by the
Indians. The problem is that natural right has no practical meaning
outside political society of a certain kind. Outside those limits, there
is nothing but the rule of force and on that level the Indian culture
cannot survive. Harsh as it seems, Tocqueville's description of the
contest between Reds and Whites supports what Mr. Bell says in
behalf of American policy.

> . . . the practice of buying Indian titles is but the substitute which
> humanity and expediency have imposed, in the place of the sword
> in arriving at the actual enjoyment of property claimed by the
> right of discovery, and sanctioned by the natural superiority al-
> lowed to the claims of civilized communities over those of savage
> tribes.[8]

This harsh conclusion might have been avoided if the Whites
had resisted their own greed for land and preserved something of
independence for the Indian nations through the exercise of their
own self- control. But Tocqueville shows that that would have been
impossible. In another footnote he cites the examples of the conflict
between the Americans and the French Canadians and Mexicans,
and he shows that the situation is similar. He concludes that, "If
comparatively imperceptible differences in European civilization
lead to such results, it is easy to see what must happen when the
most fully developed civilization of Europe comes into contact with
Indian barbarism."[9] Thus, the conflict between the Indians and
the Whites is as inevitable as the outcome of that conflict.

These reflections are not intended to exculpate or to excuse
the Whites of the injustice of their extermination of the Indian
culture, and even Indian people. That Whites cannot now atone
for their crime, nor could they have prevented themselves from
committing it, does not mean that the crime was not theirs. As in
the doctrine of original sin, may we not be guilty of a crime we
know not how to prevent or retribute—guilty in our very natures?
The rhetorical effect of chapter 10 is to enhance the feeling of guilt
among Whites, and not to excuse it. Tocqueville's reflections on the

origin of American White society would weaken the capacity of that society to honor justice if it excused the necessary injustice in that origin. The effect of Tocqueville's discussion of the Reds and the Whites in America is to temper Americans' pride with guilt.

From the more particular perspective of the legislator, the criminality at the origin of American society has another, additional significance. He sees that the necessity of the criminality of the origin of American society extends to every society coming into existence that can be imagined. While we understand that every successful society must honor the forms of justice, we see that justice is not the most comprehensive standard of political life. It is not nature's own standard. Tocqueville's discussion of the Reds and Whites illustrates poignantly the Machiavellian formula, all too easily mouthed without feeling, that nature endorses success. Can nature be so perverse as to conspire against the triumph of her own most precious flower? Because Tocqueville shares Machiavelli's view on this fundamental point, he ultimately has been able to recognize democracy as a tyranny, necessarily repressive of certain rare but fine things in the human soul, and still not take this as a decisive reason for resisting it. Tyranny or no, democracy is proved to be naturally superior to the pre-democratic order because it is stronger. It proved itself more consistent with nature's ordinances, written into the very structure of human wants and needs. It is not that the Whites have transcended pride, but only that there is a democratic form of pride that the Whites have that is superior to the Indians' because it does not make a debilitating distinction between workers and warriors. The pre-democratic form of pride was self-defeating, the democratic pride is self-vindicating; and that is the core of the inevitable triumph of democracy. One could even say, as Tocqueville does say, that God Himself has willed it so, and thereby put the Machiavellian formula in a politely pious plane. This is appropriate provided, as Tocqueville does provide, that one holds that God helps those who help themselves.

Tocqueville continues his examination of the three races in the United States by examining the relationship between Blacks and Whites primarily in the American south. He shows the horrible consequences of the violation of the fundamental principle of human equality through the institution of Negro slavery. What he says only confirms what was indicated in the discussion of the Reds. He notes that there is a difference between slavery as practiced by ancient peoples and modern slavery. As if to illustrate his earlier remark that civilized societies must *contest* the rights that pre-civilized peoples simply violate, Tocqueville says that slavery among the ancients was based simply and openly upon the military force of the conqueror over a conquered people. Unlike modern slavery, there was no implication of racial inferiority in the slave that could make the slavery just. While the comparison between the ancient and modern worlds is not flattering to the ancients, the practical effects of modern slavery are more nearly indelible and more devastating both to the slave and to the master where the presumption of racial superiority necessarily operates to assuage the more sensitive modern conscience.

> In antiquity the most difficult thing was to change the law; in the modern world the hard thing is to alter mores, and our difficulty begins where theirs ended.[10]

The evil of modern slavery is deepened by the racial inferiority in the slave that it necessarily implies, and Tocqueville describes the dimensions of *that* problem in the starkest and most pessimistic terms.

> Hitherto whenever the Whites have been more powerful they have kept the Negroes down in degradation or in slavery. Everywhere the Negroes have been stronger, they have destroyed the Whites; and that is the only reckoning there has ever been between the two races.
>
> Race prejudice seems stronger in those states that have abolished slavery than in those where it still exists, and nowhere is it more intolerant than in those states where slavery was never known.[11]

While Tocqueville displays a genuine sympathy for the plight of the Blacks under slavery,[12] his chief concern is with the effects of these influences on Whites. He shows that Whites in the south begin to take on the same contempt for labor, and the glorification of hunting and war characteristic of feudal nobles,and as a result the White civilization is weakened.[13] Most curious of all is the statement that the Whites in the south are aware of the diseconomy of slavery and its harmful social effects. "Increasing enlightenment in the South makes the people there see that slavery is harmful to the master."[14] The contrast in the productivity of labor and of the economy itself between free states is not lost on southerners. Nevertheless, the southern Whites seem incapable of ridding themselves of the millstone around their necks. "The same enlightenment makes them see, more clearly than they had seen it before, that it is almost impossible to abolish it...Slavery is more and more entrenched in the laws just where its utility is most contested."[15] The southerners are aware of the effects of their prejudice without being free of it—and they know that the abolition of slavery would not mean an end to racism. They are enlightened enough to see that an abolition of slavery would mean an open conflict between the races that would likely spell the end of White civilization, and faced with the alternative of a gradually weakening economy and cultural extinction, they choose the former. Could they in fact transcend their racial prejudice entirely, the problem would vanish, but that is scarcely to be expected. In fact, the unflattering opinion Whites have toward Blacks has some justification. The Blacks are backward; and the barrier to racial integration that that fact creates is not less formidable because it is a consequence of prejudice itself. In a footnote, Tocqueville succinctly summarizes the problem that the southerners have allowed to develop so as to leave little room for hope. "To induce the Whites to abandon the opinion they have conceived of the intellectual and moral inferiority of their former slaves, the Negroes must change, but they cannot change so long as this opinion exists."[16]

As a result of his analysis of the effects of slavery on American society, Tocqueville is led to the conclusion that the union among the states will probably fail. "The present Union will last only so long as all the states composing it wish to remain a part thereof,"[17] and that will not be long. The divisive effects of slavery are not countervailed by any real *bond* among American states. It is not that the states have no interest in union. Tocqueville thinks that the issues over which the states conceive different interests are not fundamental, and they are outweighed by stronger interests in remaining united. "Southerners must wish to preserve the Union so that they should not face the Blacks alone, and the westerners must desire it so that they should not be shut up within central America without free communication with the outside world. The North too does not want the Union broken up, for it wishes to remain the connecting link between this great body and the rest of the world."[18] Nevertheless, mutual interests are not ever sufficient to form a durable political bond. What is lacking is any common affection for the Union as a nation, and without that the prospects are necessarily dim. It is in this context that Tocqueville delivers the remark that he has, "no confidence in that calculated patriotism which is founded on interest and which a change of interests may destroy.... What keeps a great number of citizens under the same government is much less a reasoned desire to remain united than an instinctive and, in a sense, involuntary accord which springs from like feelings and similar opinions."[19] Slavery destroys that "accord" among the Americans, despite so much else that they have in common. "In the South slavery has not created interests opposed to those of the North, but it has modified the character of the southerners and given them different customs.... Slavery therefore does not attack the American confederation directly, through interests, but indirectly, through mores."[20]

The dim prospects for the survival of the American union do not, however, cause Tocqueville to be pessimistic about the future of republican government in America. On the contrary, it is almost a certainty that Americans will continue to enjoy the advantages of freedom in democracy at least in the north.[21] This confident prediction would be surprising if it were stated at the end of Part I of the first volume, because in Part I it rather appeared that the federal union was the institution whereby American republicanism was preserved from the tendency towards democratic centralism in the states. But coming at the end of Part II, Tocqueville's confidence in the future of American republicanism despite the probable collapse of the federal union is less surprising, for we have been brought to see more clearly how the political institutions are more symptoms than causes of American political health. The root cause of the American ability to preserve freedom against the dangers of democracy is their good mores, or in other words their civic virtues, and those virtues belong to a structure that is comprehensible on the level of the civil religion.

> In the United States republicans value mores, respect beliefs, and recognize rights. They hold the view that a nation must be moral, religious and modest all the more because it is free. In the United States, 'republic' means the tranquil reign of the majority. The majority, when it has time to examine itself and prove its standing, is the common source of every power. But even there the majority is not all powerful. Humanity, justice, and reason stand above it in the moral order; and in the world of politics acquired rights take precedence over it. The majority recognizes these limits,

and if it does break through them, that is because, like any man, it has passions and, like him, may do evil knowing what is good.[22]

We have had the occasion to observe Tocqueville's "Rousseauism" earlier. By this point we can see how that influence accounts for the overall structure of the first volume of *Democracy in America*. Both writers start from the idea that the fullest enjoyment of freedom that is possible for mankind is possible only on the level of social and political equality. Whereas Tocqueville takes for granted the irresistible influence of the idea of equality Rousseau labors to establish the natural grounds of equality—but both Tocqueville and Rousseau hold equality to be of the same value in connection with political freedom. Tocqueville follows Rousseau in holding that genuine political freedom requires more than that government be thought legitimate as deriving from the implicit consent of the governed. They maintain that it requires active and direct self-government by the people themselves. Both Tocqueville and Rousseau are driven to the consideration of federalism, since direct popular rule is possibly only within a small compass, while the requirements of security make large nations necessary. In the *Social Contract*, Rousseau breaks off the discussion of federalism almost before it begins in earnest with the remark that that subject would require another volume; and the reader is left with a great question unanswered.[23] Tocqueville does develop the discussion of federalism, but his development goes far enough for us to see that there is no formally sufficient answer to the question of the separation of powers between the provincial and the central government that answers both the need for active self-government and strong and effective central government. Both writers then shift their attention to the issue of mores and the civil religion, since where these things are right, the people can reap the benefits and avoid the pitfalls of differing institutions. The account of the civil religion itself as a common faith that God smiles on each man who respects the sanctity of other men's rights and is tolerant of other men's convictions is held by both Tocqueville and Rousseau to answer the spiritual needs of mankind at large and to do so in a way that contributes to the health of the political community.

The final solution to the problem of democracy on the level of democracy is, in a word, the "general will." If Tocqueville does not actually use that expression, his whole analysis points to it. As Rousseau said, the general will does not exist if it does not act; there needs to be some medium—a ritual, so to speak—through which the idea of the common life can be acted out by the citizens. The idea of the general will is not in itself the grounds for the *specific*, actual form that it will take, however. Rousseau indicates, near the end of Book 2 of the *Social Contract*, that a variety of forms are possible: the Hebrews and the Arabs each developed a ritual around their religion itself, the Athenians studied and produced literature, the Carthaginians and Tyrians practiced commerce, and the Romans and Spartans devoted themselves to war and valor.[24] Now, at the very conclusion of the last chapter of Volume I of his book, Tocqueville describes how Americans practice commerce, and in the light of the general connection between Tocqueville and Rousseau it seems clear that commerce has become the form of the American general will.

> What the French did for the sake of victory (the Americans) are doing for the sake of economy.
>
> An American navigator leaves Boston to go and buy tea in China. He arrives at Canton, stays a few days there, and comes back. In less than two years he has gone around the whole globe, and only once has he seen land. Throughout a voyage of eight or ten months he has drunk brackish water and eaten salted meat; he has striven continually against the sea, disease, and boredom; but on his return he can sell tea a farthing cheaper than an English merchant can: he has attained his aim.
>
> I cannot express my thoughts better than by saying that the Americans put something heroic into their way of trading.[25]

Tocqueville closes the last chapter of Volume I with this description of the heroic spirit with which Americans conduct commerce. It is an appropriate conclusion to a chapter properly described as being about things specifically American rather than about democracy itself or even about democracy as it exists in America, for non-democratic as well as democratic nations have made commerce the medium of their common life. It is also a fitting conclusion to a book that has more than America as its theme and aims to present a science of the characteristics and needs of democracy itself. Tocqueville's description of the commercial greatness of the Americans illustrates that the democratic legislator must sound the particular characteristics of his own nation in order to give motion and life to the political body. With this recognition, Tocqueville joins Rousseau in bowing to the example of Montesquieu.

Five

The Intellectual Disposition of Democratic Individuals

Volume II, Book 1

When Volume II of *Democracy in America* was published five years after Volume I, it was much less enthusiastically received.[1] This is understandable; Volume II is more subjective than Volume I. In Volume II Tocqueville makes more prominent the necessarily speculative theme of democracy itself rather than democracy in America. To the European audience, eager for hard data about American institutions, Volume II may have been something of a disappointment. Moreover, the purpose of Volume II is somewhat unclear. Why is it conjoined to Volume I? Had it not been written, Volume I would still have been an important book, and it would have been recognized as a finished product. It does not leave unresolved questions or half-developed points that require a continuation. Is Volume II merely a compilation of personal notes— Tocqueville's speculative reflections on democracy and America that were left over from the more tightly controlled presentation of facts and conclusions in Volume I?

Tocqueville's own stated view is that, even if Volume I could stand alone, the two volumes should be read as two parts to a single work.[2] The specific relationship that the two parts stand towards one another is worth a moment's reflection. An overview of each volume separately reveals that Volume I has as its specific theme the democratic regime; it deals with institutions and with the character of the "democratic sovereign" treated quite purposefully as a collective being. Volume II on the other hand treats individuals in democracy; their opinions, feelings, and habits or mores. As Volume I is about the regime, Volume II is about the soul. The relationship between Volumes I and II of *Democracy in America* is at least one of parallelism, following the parallel that Plato observes between the regime and the soul in the Republic. I suggest that Tocqueville is fully aware of what is implied by the parallel between the regime and the soul that Plato had interpreted so forcefully, and he means to accept it. It is not by virtue of this parallel that it can make sense to talk, as Tocqueville does, of a collective being comprising many individuals, who has "instincts and passions" of his own and who has virtue but is subject to vice like any man?[3] The relation between the regime and the soul, whereby it is as if the regime *had* a soul, is not simply a literary conceit—if it is a metaphor it is the metaphor by which the idea of common life is possible. Tocqueville has shown in Volume I that without that idea, there can be no genuine political bond.[4] One way of summarizing Tocqueville's rejection of those false champions of modernity "whose object it is to make men materialists,"[5] is to say that in their attempt to generate social order out of the material interest that individuals have, they ignore that dimension of the soul by which we participate in the life of a social body.

Tocqueville is aware that the relationship between the regime and the soul is merely a parallel, and that it is imperfect. The "instincts and passions" of the democratic sovereign, the majority, are not exactly the same as the instincts and passions of the typical democratic citizen; they are derivative, and therefore they require separate treatment. Volume II is a necessary part of *Democracy in America* to the extent that one should not take too literally the suggestion that the democratic sovereign is an individual. It was possible and useful to think in terms of the instincts and passions of the majority as a collective being in Volume I because of the facts about the character of democratic individuals that Tocqueville perceives but which operated only implicitly in Volume I.

Volume II extends to another important dimension of the analysis of democracy, that of the character of the individual democratic citizen. This is not to say that Volume II is more fundamental than Volume I however. Indeed, as Volume II develops, from the description of the opinions of democratic citizens in Book 1, through feelings in Book 2, and finally to the *mores* of democratic citizens in Book 3, the discussion becomes steadily more political. We are drawn back to the horizon of Volume I as our attention is focused on democratic mores. This is to be expected, for in the way Tocqueville uses the term, mores are a sort of second nature that men come to assume as a result of living in civil society of a certain kind. Mores are the voice of the nation in the soul of the individual. If Volume II colors in the details about democratic individuals that might have been oversimplified in the description of the instincts and passions of the majority, those details would leave an incomplete picture until they are seen as extensions, and even derivations from the character of the collective being. Man's second nature is as much a derivation from his common life as the common life is an extension of the life of the social individual. To treat either term as more fundamental than the other always leaves something incomplete.

The first book of Volume II presents an account of the opinions that are characteristic of Americans, and shows how those opinions are related to the general disposition of mind that characterizes democratic citizens in general. Tocqueville's first observation in this connection is that the Americans have thoroughly adopted the method of Descartes. They have little regard for the authority of tradition or established rules and procedures and prefer to resolve all their problems by relying on their own unaided reason. The Americans' Cartesianism in this loose sense does not derive from their having read Descartes' works and having been persuaded by them; indeed Americans scarcely know Descartes' name or that there is any issue regarding the rational acceptability of his method. "The Americans never read Descartes' works because their state of society distracts them from speculative inquiries, and they follow his precepts because this same state of society naturally leads them to adopt them."[6] The Americans are in the habit of thinking for themselves. Tocqueville gives two reasons to explain this highly flattering account of American intellectual activity. First, the social and political state of the Americans gives them the constant opportunity to exercise their minds to meet the practical requirements of life. As Tocqueville showed in the first part of Volume I, the Americans do not suffer from the effects of a system of central administration that removes the inconveniences from the life of the individual without causing him even to pay them any attention.[7] Second, Americans make good use of the Cartesian method because they do not carry it too far. They are not led into what would become paralyzing doubt in the realm of great philosophical and theological questions that are not resolvable through the application of reason to personal experience alone. The reason for this, Tocqueville says, is the strength of Christianity among Americans. "Since the Americans have accepted the main dogmas of the Christian religion without examination, they are bound to receive in like manner a great number of moral truths derived therefrom and attached thereto. This puts strict limits on the field of action left open to individual analysis and keeps out of this field many of the most important subjects about which men can have opinions."[8]

It would seem that the Americans are able to put the Cartesian method to good use because they know when not to use it. But that is an explanation that succeeds only in begging the question. *The question is, how are the Americans able to observe so clearly the subtle line that marks off the sphere where traditional authority of Christianity rules from the sphere that is left open to individual investigation and reason?* To say that the Americans allow their minds to be governed by the two different forms of authority does not explain how they avoid the potential conflict between them.

The answer to this question is that Christianity, or at least what is meant by Christianity among the Americans, sets its own limits. To see just how that operates, it is necessary to look at religion from a human point of view, as Tocqueville did in Chapter 9 of Part II, in Volume I, so as to see what is the necessary role of religion in human affairs and how American democracy submits to that necessity. What Tocqueville says is perfectly consistent with what he had said in Volume I. Religion is necessary because there are some questions about which men cannot help abut wonder but which cannot be investigated profitably. "No philosopher in the world, however great, can help believing things on trust from others or assuming the truth of many things besides those he has proved."[9] That there be some unquestioned intellectual authority is then not only a social necessity, but it is more deeply a psychological one from which none can escape. The important question is not, therefore, whether a man puts trust in unproven ideas, but in which ideas and from what source.[10] "Thus men who live in times of equality find it hard to place the intellectual authority to which they submit, beyond and outside humanity. Generally speaking, they look into themselves or into their fellows for the sources of truth." Tocqueville notes parenthetically in this connection that because democratic peoples are so absolutely governed by generally held beliefs, no new religion is likely to be established among them.[11] If Tocqueville's argument leads to any recommendations concerning religion in democracy, those recommendations will have to operate within the constraint that the contemporary forms that Christianity has assumed cannot be successfully attacked and supplanted.

Tocqueville esentially observes that the authoritative source of religion in American democracy, as in all democracies, is public opinion. The majority opinion exerts "a mighty pressure of the mind of all upon the intelligence of each [and] it imposes its ideas and makes them penetrate men's very souls."[12] In the near future the power of public opinion will be on the increase, so that "it is safe to foresee that trust in common opinion will become a sort of religion, with the majority as its prophet."[13] Where men do not have the strength or wit to inquire, they must trust; and in democracy what they trust is popular opinion. They trust it not *because* the popular opinion accords with their own, but instinctively, because they trust that *whatever* the popular opinion is it will be right, even without their taking the trouble to find out what that opinion might happen to be on any particular point. Under this thesis, it is understandable why reason and trust do not conflict in America. The Americans have a sort of unthinking though experienced trust in the sufficiency of their own private reason in dealing with their practical affairs; and they simply do not turn their minds to those great and fundamental questions where their confidence would wither. The strength of Christianity among the Americans amounts to the unflappable sanguinity that theological matters will take care of themselves since they do not seem to trouble the majority.

In presenting the power of public opinion in this way, Tocqueville cannot help but recognize that it poses a threat to genuine intellectual freedom. He makes a statement worthy of John Stuart Mill about the dangers of the despotism of popular opinion. "For myself, if I feel the hand of power heavy on my brow, I am little concerned to know who it is that oppresses me; I am no better inclined to pass my head under the yoke because a million men hold it for me."[14] But this noble expression should not obscure the difference between Tocqueville and Mill regarding the power of popular opinion. Tocqueville insists that the power of popular opinion in democracy is an irresistible fact and only the form that it takes is open to modification. Tocqueville is not a liberal of Mill's stripe. He does not make an argument that aims to preserve a wide and interesting variety of opinions among men regarding fundamental issues. He accepts without a whimper that such a variety is impossible in democracy, and in view of his understanding of the importance of such opinions to human well being, his willingness to accept the conventionalism of democratic men is understandable.[15]

For Tocqueville, what is important to the preservation of such intellectual freedom as it is possible for men to enjoy is the form that public opinion takes. The issue here is exactly the same as the issue of how the political authority of the majority will rule. Will the vice of democratic centralism destroy that limited liberty on the provincial level whereby men can in fact exercise some control over their affairs, or will such liberty be honored? In the intellectual world, the vice of democratic centralism is described by Tocqueville as a penchant for generalizations and inattention to important details.

> With us, on the other hand, there seems to have developed such an unrestrained passion for generalizations that it must, in whatever context, be satisfied. I wake every morning to be told that some general and eternal law of which I have never heard before has just been discovered.[16]

The problem that Tocqueville does address in the remainder of Book 1 is how might democratic citizens resist this slovenliness of mind that robs them of the potential intellectual virtues that they could have.

The reason that democratic citizens are given to generalizations is not primarily that they have too little time for anything else. More fundamentally, they are comfortable with generalizations of all sorts *because they are in the habit of viewing themselves and other people under a single generalization.*

> When standards are very far from equal and the inequalities are permanent, individuals gradually become so dissimilar that one can almost talk of as many types of humanity as there are classes. Attention is never fixed on more than one of these at the same time, and losing sight of the connecting thread which links them all within the vast bosom of mankind, it is invariably not man but certain men who are observed. Members, therefore, of aristocratic societies never make grand generalizations about themselves, and that is enough to give them a habitual distrust and unconscious distaste for all generalizations.
>
> Contrariwise, the democratic citizen sees nothing but people more or less like himself around him, and so he cannot think about one branch of mankind without widening his view until it includes the whole.... Having acquired a taste for generalizations in the matters which most closely take up his attention and touch is interests, he carries it with him when dealing with everything else.[17]

This is a critically important point for the argument in the first book of Volume II, because even though Tocqueville wants democracy to be more attentive to details that interfere with generalizations, the intellectual disposition that causes men to catch mankind under a single, generalized idea must be understood as a great advantage. Democracy's penchant for often overly facile generalizations is an extension of the emergence of the idea of humanity itself, which is the great force in the modern world. It is in this context that Tocqueville delivers the statement quoted earlier in this interpretation, that "The Profoundest and most wide-seeing minds of Greece and Rome never managed to grasp the very general but very simple conception of the likeness of all men and of the equal right of all at birth to liberty."[18] Aristocratic subjects saw men as different, even unique, individuals, but they did not see them as essentially equal in their natures and in their rights. Democratic citizens see the essential equality among men, but they tend to lose sight of their individuality. Tocqueville says that God would see both: mankind at large and at the same time each individual man; but men do not have God's ability, and they rely on general ideas when they cannot comprehend at once the actual individuals.[19] The mind of man is always defective, but not always in the same way, and as between the aristocratic versus the democratic limitation, the democratic one is to be preferred. Democracy can be so organized that the citizens will come to pay attention to at least those details that are important within the sphere where they govern their own lives. But aristocracy's blindness to the idea of humanity cannot be overcome except by the displacement of aristocratic society with democracy.

Having identified the intellectual strength and the weakness characteristic of democratic citizens, Tocqueville turns in chapters 5 through 8 to a discussion of religion. The discussion is basically consistent with what he had written in the ninth chapter of the second part of Volume I, except that here he is particularly concerned with the question of how religion might aid in causing democratic citizens to resist the temptation to think in terms of over-generalizations. The religious dogma that democracy will be able to accept must be simple, clear, and authorative.[20] In addition to this, religion in democracy must meet one other requirement; it must be permissive of those little, self-serving activities with which men are busy most of the time.

A passion for well-being is, as we shall see, the most lively of all
the emotions aroused or inflamed by equality, and it is a passion
shared by all. So this taste for well-being is the most striking and
unalterable characteristic of democratic ages. It may be that, should
any religion attempt to destroy this mother of all desires, it would
itself be destroyed thereby.[21]

The obvious question is how is it possible for a religion to be both
authoritative and permissive? Must not the authority of traditional
Christian religion necessarily extend to rules for moral behavior,
specifically restraining the passion for "well-being" on the grounds
that spiritual affairs take precedence over bodily desires? Does the
requirement that modern religion permit the pursuit of private
gain not necessarily conflict with Christianity's identification of the
sin of greed? Tocqueville attempts to deflect this question by re-
sorting to the theme he raised in Volume I, that religion must
operate within a different sphere from the secondary affairs of this
world.

My answer is that one must make a careful distinction between
the chief opinions which form a belief, and are what the theo-
logians call articles of faith, and those secondary notions which
are connected with it. Religions are bound to hold firmly to the
first, whatever may be the spirit of the time. But they should be
very careful not to bind themselves like that to the secondary
ones at a time when everything is in flux and the mind, accustomed to the moving pageant of human affairs, is reluctant to
be held fixed.[22]

But this statement fails to resolve the difficulty. How is the line
between things regulated by faith and things belonging to the world
of flux to be drawn? If religion must yield whenever its precepts
contend against the political wisdom of tolerating and even encouraging strong passions, religion becomes an authority that is
honored only in the breach. How can there be a dividing line
between the two forms of authority, especially in democracy where

The concept of unity has become an obsession. Man looks for it
everywhere, and when he thinks he has found it, he gladly reposes
in that belief. Not content with the discovery that there is nothing
in the world but one creation and one Creator, he is still embar-
rassed by this primary division of things and seeks to expand

and simplify his conception by including God and the universe in one great whole.[23]

The religion that poses these questions most critically is Catholicism. Tocqueville says that Catholicism is likely to be strong in democracy just because the authority of the Catholic Church is uniform and absolute.[24] Everybody is treated as equal before the altar. Then, seemingly continuing the account of Catholicism's advantages, Tocqueville adds a paragraph that on reflection raises the problem of the limitedness of its authority.

> One of the most familiar weaknesses of the human mind is to want to buy peace at the cost of logic. So there are now and always will be some people who, having submitted to authority in some of their religious beliefs, still seek to exempt some of their other beliefs from it and let their minds float at random between obedience and freedom. But I am disposed to believe that their number will be fewer in democratic ages than at other times and that our grandchildren will tend more and more to be divided clearly between those who have completely abandoned Christianity and those who have returned to the church of Rome.[25]

Within the sphere of religion Catholicism comports with democracy's instinct for unity because it answers every question under one simple authority and tolerates no compromise. But what about the duality between religion and political authority? Is not this an example of buying peace at the cost of logic? In view of this difficulty, and what follows in the next two chapters of *Democracy in America*, the concluding sentence of the passage quoted above might be restated in a way less flattering to Catholicism. It is likely that many people will accept the absolute authority of the Church of Rome since it holds all men to one set of rules without regard for their differences. But the fundamental duality between the authority of the Church and the political authority will necessarily lead many others to abandon traditional Christianity altogether in favor of a religion more directly compatible with the nature of political authority. It deserves mention at this point too that, because of the resistance among democratic citizens to new religions of any sort, the last thing of Christianity that is likely to be abandoned will be the name.[26]

Tocqueville has shown that it is a mistake to think that those who gravitate away from the Church of Rome in the future will not have anything in the way of a systematic view of man and nature; there is always some comprehensive notion about such matters to which the mind attaches. The next two chapters of *Democracy in America* appear to set forth two radical alternatives, other than Catholicism, that are open to democracy: Pantheism, and "the idea of the indefinite perfectibility of man." Tocqueville expresses open hostility towards the doctrine of Pantheism. It is an evil doctrine because it "destroys human individuality, [and] just because it destroys it, will have secret charms for men living under democracies."[27] Pantheism can be understood as the doctrine that represents, on the level of religion, the extreme example of democracy's penchant for generalization at the expense of individuals. It reduces men to the status of interchangeable elements in a great flux, where only permanence and rank are forbidden.

An interpretation is necessary, in the form of a public teaching about the order of the world and man's place within it that comports with democracy's instinct for a simple and general rule while at the same time supporting the idea of the individual and his freedom. I suggest it is in response to this need that Tocqueville addresses the chapter immediately following his indictment of Pantheism, "How Equality Suggests to the Americans the Idea of the Indefinite Perfectibility of Man."

> Though man resembles the animals in many respects, one characteristic is peculiar to him alone; he improves himself and they do not.... So the idea of perfectibility is as old as the world, equality had no share in bringing it to birth, but it has given it a new character.
>
> When citizens are classified by rank, profession, or birth, and when all are obliged to follow the career which chance has opened before them, everyone thinks that he can see the ultimate limits of human endeavor quite close in front of him, and no one attempts to fight against the inevitable fate. It is not that aristocratic peoples absolutely deny man's capacity to improve himself, but they do not think it unlimited. They think in terms of amelioration, not change.... they assume in advance certain impassable limits to such progress....
>
> But when castes disappear and classes are brought together, when men are jumbled together and habits, customs, and laws are changing, when new facts impinge and new truths are discovered, when old conceptions vanish and new ones take their place, then the human mind imagines the possibility of an ideal but always fugitive perfection....

> Thus, searching always, falling, picking himself up again, often disappointed, never discouraged, he is ever striving toward that immense grandeur glimpsed indistinctly at the end of the long track humanity must follow.[28]

The discussion of the doctrine of human perfectibility shows that this idea opposes the bad consequences of Pantheism, but it does not do so as traditional Christianity does, through recourse to a dualism between the mundane and the transworldly realms. The idea of indefinite perfectibility seems to deny the significance of any transworldly perfection—any "ideal" human nature to which no individual human being can perfectly correspond. According to the doctrine of perfectibility, the essence of human nature is a kind of openness.

From the standpoint of rationality, this notion of indefinite perfectibility is subject to a host of questions and objections. There seems to be a fundamental confusion in it between the potentiality and the actuality of human nature. But Tocqueville makes no attempt to give a rational defense for the doctrine. He says only that it accords with democracy's intellectual propensities *and* that it has the enormous practical advantage of giving sanction to the notion of freedom. The idea of indefinite perfectibility sanctions a *vision* of society wherein each man, through the pursuit of the betterment of his own material conditions, sees himself contributing to a more general advance and that he thus partakes of "the natural greatness of man." Indefinite perfectibility is the doctrine that ennobles the indefinite progress in material well-being to which democracy gives license, and thus it is "the general and systematic conception by which a great people conducts all its affairs."

> I once met an American sailor and asked him why his country's ships are made so they will not last long. He answered offhand that the art of navigation was making such progress that even the best of boats would be almost useless if it lasted more than a few years.[29]

Properly set forth, the doctrine of human perfectibility yields to democracy a vision of itself that can enlarge the heart and can provide sanction and opportunity for noble exertions. While democracy can only value the labor of the mind if it produces material goods, this need not mean that the status of the intelligence is thereby demeaned. It will not be demeaned if men can be brought to interpret material improvement as the *sign* of the greatness of human nature.[30] It is just because knowledge is seen by democracy to be useful that "no one easily allows himself to be confined to the material cares of life, and the humblest artisan occasionally casts an eager, furtive glance at the higher regions of the mind."[31] I interpret Tocqueville's discussion of the doctrine of the indefinite perfectibility of man to be the cardinal element of a public philosophy or civil religion whereby he transforms democratic envy that "leads the weak to want to drag the strong down," into a healthy and proudful belief that one shares in a political order that reveals the natural greatness of man. The resulting pride is what Tocqueville means both by the manly love of equality and by the spirit of freedom.

In Chapters 9 through 21 of Book 1, Tocqueville shows what talents and shortcomings democratic citizens are likely to have in various fields of intellectual activity. He asserts that the dearth of science, literature, and art in America is not indicative of a general failing of democratic citizens. America is poor by these measures of culture because she is by and large a wilderness, not because of democracy.[32] Democratic citizens can be expected to appreciate the value of intellectual activity and knowledge *more* than those things were appreciated by men in aristocratic times, precisely because in democracy everyone sees the utility of knowledge towards their own personal well being. Even though democracy lacks a leisured few who spend their time exclusively in intellectual activity and who may produce monuments to their own personal intellectual powers, democracy gains because more people are involved in little ways in the practical part of science, so that "as in the political life of the United States; . . . the attempts are innumerable; and though each individual achievement is generally very small, the total effect is always very great."[33]

The problem with this sanguine view, though, is that democratic citizens are not so likely to give their attention to the higher realms of intellectual activity where the utility is less immediate.[34] Under aristocracy, there were always a few who valued knowledge simply for its own sake. Tocqueville cites the example of Archimedes, who had such an "inconsiderate contempt" for utility that he refused to write any description of instruction about how to reconstruct the machines of war by which he helped defend Syracuse against the Roman invaders.[35] The advancement of learning depends upon research and thought at the level of theory, and Tocqueville admits that democracy does not give the spur to that sort of activity.

Despite the problem that democratic citizens tend to be interested in those branches of science where the payoff is quickest, Tocqueville thinks that when the final tally is taken, science will advance more impressively under democracy than aristocracy. Tocqueville calls for an effort, presumably by institutions of public education, to keep men interested in theory; and it is an effort that can be made with the hope of success. "The taste itself for practice, if it is enlightened, should not lead men to neglect theory. While so many things are being tried out, with new experiments every day, it is almost impossible that very general laws should not frequently be brought to light. Great discoveries are bound to be frequent, though great discoverers may be few."[36] Both aristocracy and democracy suffer from a deficiency regarding the attitude they generate towards science, but the deficiency in aristocracy is worse. Tocqueville characterizes as "proud and sterile"[37] the aristocratic search for truth. When Tocqueville gives his own account of the structure of scientific principles, it comes to light that fundamentally he endorses the democratic conception of the *value* of truth, rather than the aristocratic conception.

> The mind, it appears to me, can divide science into three parts. The first compromises the most theoretical principles and the most abstract conceptions whose application is either unknown or very remote.
>
> The second compromises general truths which, though still based in theory, lead directly and immediately to practical application.
>
> Methods of application and means of execution make up the third.[38]

All truths belong to a single structure, from the highest and most comprehensive principles to those which bear immediately on practical issues. There is no disjunction, in other words, between a practical as versus a wholly contemplative realm of truth. Tocqueville shares the democratic presumption that science is to be pursued for the sake of relieving the human estate. There remains only the question of causing democratic citizens to be farsighted enough to limit their present enjoyments in order to invest the effort necessary to foster still greater enjoyments in the future.

Perhaps the greatest cause of the disappointment that some men will always feel about the way democracy values the works of the mind remains: the question whether in democracy there can ever be that inducement to the *way of life* that is spent in the pursuit of the truth itself, whatever its value to the generality of men. In a way, the inegalitarian structure of aristocratic society points towards such a life as *the* life that contains the final answer to the question of the point of human life as such. There is a kind of resolution of the troublesome question of the meaning of human life that is contained in the idea that the truth is a value beyond all utility to be pursued for itself alone. Comforted by that formulation, even the majority of men who do not have the gifts for the life of the mind might be expected to find some happiness in their station, confident that what they do contributes to a social structure that at some point exhibits the full measure of human being. Democracy, disturbingly, offers no such comfort; it does not reflect any rank of human activities that leads up to any one way of life that is viewed as fully human. Tocqueville is aware of this. He is genuinely awed by the example of Pascal, whom he describes as having burned himself out before the age of forty in the selfless pursuit of the "hidden secrets of the Creator."[39] While the honor that Tocqueville pays to Pascal cannot be read without a sense of sadness and even bitterness when we realize that if Pascal were alive today he would evoke only puzzled curiosity, nevertheless Tocqueville makes two observations in this context that prevent him from attacking democracy. First, awesome as is the example of Pascal, it is not one that it would be sensible for men to try to imitate out of envy for the praise that Pascal deserves. While the love of the truth might draw another to do what Pascal did, it would not be to win applause. If men were to have the example of Pascal before them and so be tempted to imitate him from motives of ambition, it would only lead to deep frustration and fanaticism. The other point is connected with the first; when we understand the true character of the motives that moved Pascal, it appears that such men may exist at any time or place—so long as they are not positively repressed. They neither seek nor need society's recognition.

> Nor is it credible that among so great a multitude a speculative genius should not from time to time arise inspired by the love of truth alone. Such a one will surely penetrate the deepest mysteries of nature, whatever be the spirit of his time and place. His spirit's flight needs no help; it is enough if it is not impeded.[40]

It would be candid to acknowledge that many of Tocqueville's readers will be flatly unable to believe in the existence of such a person as Tocqueville describes Pascal to have been. The dismissal of the description of Pascal as irrelevant to the argument would make the defense of democracy's intellectual propensities all the easier. It is for those who are concerned with the prospects for philosophy under the sway of democracy that the example of Pascal is important; one sees how silly it is to try to pave the way for the one who must walk alone. Tocqueville's point is well taken: the philosopher knows how to take care of himself. The real burden of Tocqueville's book is the question of whether the more ordinary members of human society can find happiness and live in peace when there is no formal answer to the question of what makes life worth the living.

The concluding chapters of book 1 are devoted to the subjects of art and literature among democratic citizens. As art in general is the medium through which a people see themselves, the art that conforms to democracy's tastes is a reflection of all the characteristics, both virtuous and vicious, that Tocqueville has been describing as belonging to democracy throughout his book. It is also a magnification of them, especially the vices. For one thing, the absence of a leisured class that devotes itself to refined tastes and pleasures means that the works of art that please democratic citizens have to be cheap, and either useful or gaudy.[41] Such men have no instinct for delicacy or finesse; and nothing that might properly be called exquisite is likely to be produced among them. The most distressing consequence of this depravity of taste and talent is that art will come to represent only the sensible part of human nature. The democratic artist does not mold his portrait or description so as to evoke feeling for the invisible and intangible, divine element in human nature. Tocqueville mentions the name Raphael as the supreme example of that form of perfection that democratic citizens are unlikely to appreciate.[42]

By far the severest criticism of democratic art, however, is that it reinforces the tendency towards a generalizing grandiosity that dwarfs individuals.[43] Nearly everything that Tocqueville says to the discredit of democratic art and literature illustrates this general problem. For example, he shows how the Americans' construction of public monuments symbolizes a vision of the majesty of the state and the comparative insignificance of the individual. "Imagination shrinks at the thought of themselves as individuals and expands beyond all limits at the thought of the state."[44] This failing extends to literature both as to the *themes* that are chosen and to the very language itself that democratic writers use. Typically, democratic writers, "inflate their imaginations and swell them out beyond bounds, so that they achieve gigantism, missing real grandeur."[45] This pedestrian gigantism is fostered by the overuse of general terms. For example, democratic writers will use the word "capabilities" without taking the trouble to explain *of what* particular thing one is said to be capable.[46] Such words of very general significance are not only commonly used, but they are invested with the attributes of persons, and so made to stand instead of persons as the agents of actions and events. Tocqueville mockingly invents a typical democratic statement, "'the force of things will that capacities govern.'"[47] When men think in such terms they come to imagine themselves as little more than spectators to the play of forces that seem to have no human origin. Among the leading offenders are democratic historians. Tocqueville cites with approval the ancient historians such as Plutarch or Thucydides, as having made individual men the movers of events and the heroes of their stories, and thus "taught how to command; [whereas modern historians] teach next to nothing but how to obey."[48]

As we might expect, this great failing of democratic literature and art has a counterpart among aristocrats. They tend to an over refinement of taste and style which loses its connection with the permanent features of mankind everywhere.

> It will sometimes happen that men of letters, seeing none but themselves, will entirely lose sight of the rest of the world, and that will make their work farfetched and sham. They will impose petty literary rules for their exclusive use, and that will gradually make them lose first common sense and then contact with nature.
>
> Such are the natural perils for literature among aristocracies.[49]

Here as elsewhere Tocqueville is not drawing the comparison between democracy and aristocracy as if to offer his reader a choice. The choice has been made; what is important is for us to understand that democracy has certain advantages but they are distinctive and partial and come with a cost. What, then, is the best sort of art that democratic citizens are likely to produce? To answer this question Tocqueville has to reflect once again on the sources of poetic inspiration among the Americans. In the chapter that is of central importance to his whole discussion of art in democracy he warns

Europeans not to conclude that Americans have no poetry in their souls merely because their accomplishments to date have been meager.

> I gladly admit that there are no American poets, but I could not admit that Americans have no poetic ideas.... The American people see themselves marching through wildernesses, drying up marshes, diverting rivers, peopling the wilds, and subduing nature. It is not just occasionally that their imagination catches a glimpse of this magnificent vision. It is something which plays a real part in the least, as in the most important, actions of every man, and it is always flitting before his mind.
>
> There is nothing more petty, more insipid, crowded with paltry interests—in one word, antipoetic—than the daily life of an American. But among the thoughts that direct his life there is one full of poetry, and that is like a hidden sinew giving strength to the whole frame.[50]

The preservation of republican freedom is connected with the feeling that each citizen has of being part of the common life of the nation, and it is by way of this poetic vision that the citizens can feel that participation. When Tocqueville said in the last chapter of Volume I that the Americans put something heroic into their way of trading, he already implied that there was a horizon, to be drawn by poetry, for heroic efforts.

Extending his thought to democratic society in general, Tocqueville continues his description of the sources of poetic inspiration.

> In ages of democracy men are always on the move from place to place, trying to satisfy their impatient longings, and peoples of different countries mix, see one another, hear one another, and borrow from one another. So it is not only the members of a single nation that come to resemble each other; the nations themselves are assimilated, and one can form the picture of one vast democracy in which a nation counts as a single citizen. Thus for the first time all mankind can be seen together in broad daylight.
>
> The existence of the entire human race, its vicissitudes and its future, thus becomes a fertile theme for poetry.[51]

Up to a point this passage is reassuring. It might comfort those who would despair that democracy will simply lack any poetic inspiration at all; that this is a mundanely grey world in which imagination adds no luster to the chores of life and no excitement to the movements of the soul. Tocqueville says, on the contrary, that democratic citizens have lively imaginations. Their heads are constantly in the clouds, as if while plowing their fields or trading stock they hear the voice of humanity singing Beethoven's "Song of Joy." But even granting what Tocqueville says of the poetic inspiration among democratic citizens, the problem remains that their poetic image might dwarf men rather than support them. If an actual poet were to respond to this inspiration, there seems to be a danger that the theme would all too easily be exhausted in a powerful but short outpouring of artistic expression. What will provide the variety among the subjects of democratic poetry? In ages where men's attention is drawn towards individuals, there is never a lack of subject matter for new stories and new works of art. The episodes that can be imagined in the lives of individuals are infinitely varied, so that there are always fresh materials by which to move an audience to laughter or tears of sympathy when one of their kind suffers. The painter or sculptor need never lack for subjects when his eye is keen to the image of divinity in each human face. But when democratic citizens find themselves individually boring, they cannot be touched by an art that would focus on the individual for its subject.

This is the challenge for modern artists. If the artist is to retain his power, he will have to discover ways of generating *feeling* for his human subjects among a people who will too readily dismiss his characters as boring duplicates of themselves. Tocqueville thinks that such art *is* possible. He mentions Byron, Chateaubriand, and Lamartine as examples of poets who were able to make people interesting despite the ordinariness of their circumstances. They make us feel their passions even when the occasions in which those passions are expressed are not grand ones. When such a poetry exists it deserves to be called great.

> Human destiny, man himself, not tied to time or place, but face to face with nature and with God, with his passions, doubts, his unexpected good fortune, and his incomprehensible miseries, will for these peoples be the chief and almost the sole subject of poetry.[52]

Tocqueville could not have explained himself better than by referring to these three actual poets as examples of what democratic poetry can and ought to be. Their works do not belittle men; they are colorful, rich, winged, and at the same time perfectly accessible to men of ordinary experience. Nevertheless, even if these poets overcome the limitedness of democratic citizens' poetic imagination in their own art, they can not eliminate the unfortunate consequences of that limitedness for men in general. It remains true that serious poetry will not have individuals for its subject and when any sort of art treats of individuals it will not be serious. It is to this point that Tocqueville includes a rather extraordinary chapter on the theater in democracy near the end of Book 1.[53] He says that the audience of the theater understandably expects that their emotions will be touched directly by the drama. They wish to see themselves visually portrayed, almost mirrored. When aristocrats see their own lives mirrored on the stage, they see great deeds upon which the welfare of many people depend. But democratic citizens can never see themselves quite like that. The image that the theater catches of democratic life is true in a sort of direct and immediate way—in a way that cannot portray democratic citizens as other than trivial. They are the subjects of comedy far more readily than tragedy, and Tocqueville expects that democratic citizens will go to the theater to be amused, rather than moved. Because of this, Tocqueville nods his approval in the direction of the Puritan fathers who were especially hostile towards the theater. He even says that that hostility tends to persist among the Americans, "In America extreme regularity of habits and great strictness of morals have up to now told against the growth of drama ... People who spend every weekday making money and Sunday in praying to God give no scope to the muse of comedy."[54] More than any other form of art, the theater threatens the seriousness of purpose that is necessary for a well-ordered democracy. Democratic drama portrays man in bald truth; but it is the truth about the lowest part of his nature.[55]

In the final analysis, though, if one wishes to see democratic citizens giving their own best expression of their poetic imagination and their talents for moving one another in speech, one should look to the legislative assemblies. This is the stage on which men take themselves most seriously. Therefore, Book 1 concludes appropriately with a chapter on "Parliamentary Eloquence in the United States." While there are as yet no American poets of any consequence, there are great orators, and Tocqueville confesses his heartfelt praise that the whole world might listen to a sample of American political oratory for both instruction and inspiration.

. . . Europe was stirred by the first debates that took place in the little colonial assemblies of America at the time of the Revolution.

There is nothing more wonderful or more impressive than a great orator discussing great affairs in a democratic assembly. As no particular class is ever represented there by men commissioned to defend its special interests, the orator always speaks to the whole nation, for the whole nation. This heightens both his thought and his power of expression.

As precedents have little force, and there are no more privileges attached to certain property or rights inherent in certain bodies or certain men, the argument, to deal with the particular matter at hand, must be carried back to general propositions derived from the nature of humanity. For this reason, the political discussions of a democracy, no matter how small, have a general character which often attracts the interest of the human race. All men are interested because they treat of man, who is everywhere the same.[56]

Six

Democratic Citizens' *Sentiments*:

Volume II, Book 2

The second book of Volume II describes the "sentiments,"[1] i.e., feelings and passions, that are characteristic of democratic citizens. Broadly speaking, there is a great similarity between Books 2 and 1. In Book 1, Tocqueville showed that democratic citizens' whole intellectual disposition is formed by their tendency to think of themselves and others as more or less interchangeable atoms within one enormous generality—"humanity." The effort that Tocqueville calls for in Book 1 is for religion and poetry and all the other things that influence men's opinions to elevate the status of individuals in the minds of democratic citizens. The direction of effort should be towards that divine perspective from which God sees "every human being separately and sees in each the resemblances that make him like his fellows."[2] The threat of despotism is in the degree to which democratic citizens allow themselves to sink down in their own imaginations to the level of particles in one vast, undifferentiated mass. In Book 2, Tocqueville similarly describes men's emotions as being attached first and foremost to the idea of equality of all men.[3] The love of equality is, on the level of feelings or emotions, equivalent to the instinct for generalizations on the level of intellectual activity. They are the responses of the head and the heart to the revelation of "humanity" at large. In Book 2, Tocqueville shows that equality is a jealous mistress of men's emotions. Any attachments to specific people, such as one's family or countrymen, presumes a selection and so runs against the love of equality.[4] The particular loves and loyalties by which men once were able to feel the confidence and strength to resist despotism threaten to be blown away, "and there is the danger that [each man] may be shut up in the solitude of his own heart."[5] For this reason, the love of equality threatens again to atomize society and grind it into material suitable only for despotism. From this broad reflection, the discussions in Books 1 and 2 of Volume II are like two lines drawn on different planes towards one single point of intersection. One can see what Tocqueville means when he says, in his summary and concluding fourth book of Volume II, "thus two different paths have led me to the same conclusion. I have pointed out how equality prompts men to think of one sole uniform and strong government. I have just shown how equality gives them a taste for it."[6]

In the opening statement of Book 2, Tocqueville restates what is in a broad sense the controlling theme in *Democracy in America* as a whole. The love of equality is the overwhelming and incontestable fact of modern political life. Nothing that would oppose that passion can succeed. Because there are a thousand forms of political liberty that do not presume democratic equality, the love of liberty and the love of equality are two distinguishable affections; and of the two the love of equality is vastly more powerful.[7] Tocqueville gives several reasons why that is so, but in the final analysis his reasons are only so many illustrations of the raw fact that men do love equality.[8] It is simply a fact of their natures that comes out as soon as the image of humanity in general emerges clearly enough to become familiar. Tocqueville tries to show how a love of liberty might be preserved within the same heart that is dominated by the love of equality; in principle these two affections are not only compatible but also connected. It is significant that at "an extreme point freedom and equality would meet and blend." In the *perfect* expression of equality, "no man is different from his fellows, and nobody can wield tyrannical power; men will be perfectly free because they are entirely equal, and they will be perfectly equal because they are entirely free."[9] Because of this connection between equality and liberty, Tocqueville thinks that "democratic peoples have a natural taste for liberty."[10] Though the love of equality may likely destroy the conditions where liberty is possible, the fundamental connection between equality and liberty is the ultimate grounds whereby Tocqueville hopes that liberty can be preserved in democracy. It is a question of drawing out what is already implicitly present in the hearts of democratic citizens.

Tocqueville does not accuse democratic citizens of having too much self-love or "egoism." The fact that their feelings are constantly turned towards themselves derives from the social conditions of democracy—where no partial societies have sufficient durability to draw men out of themselves—and is ultimately the result of democratic jealousy.[11] This point is confirmed by the observation that, in France, where the sting of that jealousy is felt more keenly, the consequent "individualism" is an even more severe problem than it is in America.[12] Upon turning the problem this way, it is natural for Tocqueville to take up next the idea of civil associations, and "freedom of association." The argument is that, if democracy breaks down the traditional and hierarchical structures that link individuals to other people, perhaps new sorts of links among people can be contrived. Democratic citizens might voluntarily enter association with others even when they are not assigned to any particular set of personal relationships as a result of their social station. Such voluntary associations would presumably teach men the dependence of their own welfare upon that of others, and also teach them the techniques of cooperation so that the blight of "individualism" could be cured. But the apparent neatness of this cure should not cause us to accept it so readily that we fail to see why Tocqueville devotes so extended a discussion of it, nearly all of Book 2, to explain how it works. Is there not something necessarily self-defeating about the attempt to lift men up out of their individualistic feelings on the basis of an appeal to those very feelings? Why would the democratic jealousy that destroys the traditionary links among individuals not also impede the effect of voluntary associations to the extent that men's affections and loyalties begin to shift from themselves to their associations and their associates?

As one might expect, Tocqueville cites America as *the* example that voluntary associations can operate as a sort of medicine to cure the problem of democratic individualism. At first, what he says here seems to be almost a repetition of the argument he made in Part I of Volume I on administrative decentralization, and in chapter 4 of Part II of Volume I on "political association in the United States." It is a familiar thought that Tocqueville recites in the fourth chapter of Book 2, Volume II, that "local liberties, then, which induce a great number of citizens to value the affection of their kindred and neighbors, bring men constantly into contact, despite the instincts which separate them, and force them to help one another."[13] The focus of Volume II, however, is somewhat different from Volume I in a way that causes the psychological dimension of the argument to be more strongly emphasized. In Volume I, Tocqueville wanted to fashion provincial liberty and *political* associations as a bulwark against the centralizing passion of the democratic sovereign. He was concerned to show what degree of decentralization was consistent with good government in a civilized nation and what degree of freedom of political association was consistent with the requirements of the regime's security against conspiratorial threats. In Volume II, Tocqueville is more concerned with altering the feelings of individual democratic citizens towards their fellows, to teach them the habits of cooperation and trust. Therefore, in Volume II he explicitly takes up the matter of *civil* associations as distinct from political associations, observing that he had already covered only the latter.[14]

Under "civil associations" Tocqueville includes "not only commercial and industrial associations in which all take part, but a thousand different types—religious, moral, serious, futile, very general and very limited, immensely large and very minute."[15] It is in all these sorts of associations, and not only in political ones, that Americans learn to overcome individualism. It is heartening to learn that Americans profit from all the sorts of associations that they enter because that means that the salutary effects of association are much wider and more fundamental than it might have appeared otherwise. In view of the way that Tocqueville celebrates this fact, it seems that the discussion of political associations in Volume I was *too* restricted. By descending to the level of the psychology of individual democratic citizens as distinct from the instincts and passions of the collectivity, Tocqueville seems to have discovered the hopeful fact that the weakness of heart to which democratic citizens are subject can be ministered to in ways that do not threaten the majority or excite mass jealousy. Encouraging and facilitating civil associations appear to be *the* solution to the problem of democracy. The formula would be that through association for even the pettiest purposes, democratic citizens could learn the habits and acquire the strength of soul necessary and sufficient to sustain political associations, ultimately including republican institutions themselves.

As Tocqueville's discussion of associations continues, however, it becomes clear what is overlooked in the formula outlined above. The problem in general is that the destructive form of the love of equality pervades all forms of association, even civil associations, depriving men of the psychological benefits they might have derived from them. Therefore, the moderation of the destructive effects of the love of equality is more a precondition than is it the result of the political value of freedom of association. In chapters 6 and 7 of Book 2 Tocqueville examines the relationship between demo-

cratic associations and newspapers, and also the relationship between civil and political associations. These two chapters show how
the love of equality pervades and conditions the effects of even such
civil associations as democratic citizens enter for reasons of self-
interest. In the chapter on the press, Tocqueville goes further than
he did in Volume I to show why the issues of freedom of the press
and associations are linked in his mind. The central point here is
that in democracy the press is the principal medium of communication. The press maintains civilization itself among citizens who
would otherwise be totally overcome by the "menace" of individualism. Members of associations have no other medium of contact
than the press. "The leading citizens living in an aristocratic country
can see each other from afar, and if they want to unite their forces
they go to meet one another, bringing a crowd in train. But in
democratic countries [only] a newspaper gives publicity to the feeling or idea that had occurred to them all simultaneously but separately."[16] Not only do associations in democracy require newspapers,
but wherever there are newspapers they bring associations into
being, for the readership that a newspaper must have if it is to
survive can itself be thought of as an association created by the
very tool through which its members touch.

> A newspaper can only survive if it gives publicity to feelings or
> principles common to a large number of men. A newspaper there-
> fore always represents an association whose members are its reg-
> ular readers.
>
> The newspaper represents the association; one might say that it
> speaks to each of its readers in the name of all the rest, and the
> feebler they are individually, the easier it is to sweep them along.[17]

The intimate connection between associations and newspapers
has an important bearing on the argument that men can learn to
overcome individualism through voluntary associations. The reader
who shares Tocqueville's perspective on the press, that he revealed
in Volume I, will be especially keen to the implications of his observation here in Volume II. Newspapers in democracy have a built-
in egalitarian bias. The fact that in democracy newspapers are the
only means of communication means that there is a limit to what
can be conceived as the aim of a democratic association. All associations, civil as well as political, are formed under the aegis, so to
speak, of the principle of equality. Whatever an association aims to

do must be publicizable, and in democracy that means that it must not threaten democratic equality. How far this limitation constricts the freedom of association depends on the degree to which the love of equality among the citizens assumes its most jealous and destructive form.

The fact that associations in democracy are limited to the aims that are publicizable does not at first seem to be of much importance when we are considering *civil* associations. There would still be some room for optimism since democratic citizens could learn their political virtues in connection with civil associations that did not evoke democratic jealousy. But in the following chapter on the "Relationship Between Civil and Political Associations," Tocqueville adds a further consideration that poses a problem for that optimistic line of thought. Civil associations are *not* primarily the institutions through which men learn the habits of cooperation and mutual trust that they *then* use to work together for political purposes. Rather it is the other way around. "One may think of political associations as the great free schools to which all citizens come to be taught the general theory of association."[18] In civil life men fancy that they can be self-sufficient, and they are influenced by a "natural distaste for working in common."[19] Only in the realm of politics are the advantages, indeed the necessities, of working in common evident at the outset, so that men can be expected to do for a party what they are less ready to do for any other kind of mutual advantage. Thus,

> the common interests of civil life seldom naturally induce great numbers to act together. A great deal of artifice is required to produce such a result.
>
> But in politics opportunities for this are continually offering themselves of their own accord. Moreover, it is only large associations which make the general value of this method plain. Individually weak citizens form no clear conception in advance of the power they might gain by combining; to understand that, they must be shown it. Hence it is often easier to get a multitude to work together than just a few people; where one thousand do not see the advantage in combining, ten thousand do see it. In politics men combine for great ends, and the advantages gained in important matters give them a practical lesson in the value of helping one another even in lesser affairs.[20]

As an extension of this same point, Tocqueville asserts that the freedom to engage in political associations is necessary if men are to be expected to develop the general habit of association. "When citizens have the faculty and habit of associating for everything, they will freely associate for little purposes as well as great. But if they are only allowed to associate for trivial purposes, they will have neither the will nor the power to do so."[21] If this point is put together with the observation on the relationship between associations and newspapers in the preceeding chapter, what emerges is, I think, clear. Self-interest is not strong enough to lead democratic citizens into voluntary associations where political associations are instinctively looked upon as a threat to democratic equality. Democratic jealousy, enforced through the pervasively powerful instrument of the press, will crimp not only political associations, but by way of a necessary extension, *all* associations. The example of America, which *does* combat individualism by voluntary associations, begs the question as to what makes that scheme work. Tocqueville examines this further in the next several chapters, all of which deal with the "doctrine of self-interest rightly understood" as it operates in America.

The Americans have the spirit and the ability to combine their own advantage with that of others in voluntary associations in all sorts because they avow a general theory that fosters this result. The theory is that virtue is useful, so that by following one's own personal advantage intelligently, one will be led to do good. Tocqueville says that there is nothing especially new or remarkable as far as the content of this doctrine is concerned; and moreover he exhibits sublime disinterest in any discussion of the possible truth of it. He passes that off with the remark that "I do not want to follow [the Americans'] arguments in detail here, as that would lead too far from my subject."[22] What is important to him is rather that the Americans have accepted this "doctrine of self-interest rightly understood" as if it were the complete and final answer to all questions of moral philosophy and intelligent living. Tocqueville's account of the Americans' unblinking acceptance of the doctrine of self-interest rightly understood can hardly be read without a wry smile.

> The Americans, on the other hand, enjoy explaining almost every act of their lives on the principle of self-interest properly understood. It gives them pleasure to point out how an enlightened self-love continually leads them to help one another and disposes them freely to give part of their time and wealth for the good

of the state. I think that in this they often do themselves less than
justice, for sometimes in the United States, as elsewhere, one sees
people carried away by the disinterested, spontaneous impulses
natural to man. But the Americans are hardly prepared to admit
that they do give way to emotions of this sort. They prefer to give
credit to their philosophy rather than to themselves.[23]

How enlightened are these hedonists, that they would deny
themselves the pleasure of a truly generous deed rather than present an occasion whereby their public creed might prove doubtful!
So unchallenged is the doctrine of self-interest rightly understood
among the Americans that they even apply it to religion. This leads
Tocqueville to say that there is a sort of calculating spirit that is
mixed with the Americans' religious zeal. That spirit constantly
turns Americans' attention to the worldly and political value of
religion and religious morality, as something that can be more
readily weighed and compared than can one's stake in salvation.
Thus, "preachers in America are continually coming down to earth
. . . and it is often difficult to be sure when listening to them whether
the main object of religion is to procure eternal felicity in the next
world or prosperity in this."[24]

The appeal of the doctrine of self-interest rightly understood
for the Americans is readily intelligible. As Tocqueville describes
it, this sort of vulgarized utilitarianism is a highly democratic doctrine. It puts virtue within the comprehension of the pettiest of
souls, requiring nothing more than a moderate amount of good
sense to meet its standards. There is no room in this doctrine for
contempt for the baseness of the vulgar, who cannot bring themselves to care for virtue itself apart from any incidental reward. No
wonder then that the Americans accept the doctrine without question, even though it fails to provide a complete and accurate account
of their motives.

The naiveté in the Americans' acceptance of the doctrine of
self-interest rightly understood should not be taken to indicate that
genuine self-interest is not an important motive among Americans
or democratic citizens in general. Self-interest may not explain
everything as the Americans think it does, but it *is* a powerful
motive, and that is a fact that Tocqueville must acknowledge in his
account of the emotions or feelings characteristic of democratic
citizens. In democracy it is the case that men can hope to improve
their lot and their standing in society far beyond what was possible

in aristocracy through their own efforts. That fact necessarily means that they will occupy themselves nearly all of the time in the pursuit of material well-being. Tocqueville expresses his fear that ultimately democratic citizens might completely submit to busying themselves with such concerns, and that "by such means a kind of decent materialism may come to be established on earth, which will not corrupt souls but soften and imperceptibly loosen the springs of action."[25] This remark of Tocqueville's is a familiar one; its significance here in the context of the issues in Book 2 is that it raises a question about the sufficiency of the doctrine of self-interest rightly understood as the general theory by which men might be encouraged to enter voluntary associations. Even if the doctrine of self-interest rightly understood does not adequately describe all that motivates the Americans, it does encourage them to think constantly of the pursuit of materialistic satisfactions, and to harden their souls against larger emotions and more magnificent pleasures. (Tocqueville's fear of "decent materialism" indicates his own judgment that material satisfactions do not completely answer the needs of human nature or exhaust its potentialities.) We ought to expect perverse consequences when democratic citizens, almost deliberately, attempt to narrow the range of their emotions, fearing the inegalitarian implications of grand ones.

In chapters 12 and 13 Tocqueville identifies two indications that the Americans pay a psychological price for their attempt to feel nothing but the promptings of self-interest. First, he cites the wildly enthusiastic response of Americans to itinerant preachers "hawking the word of God," and says of it that "forms of religious madness are very common there."[26] Second, even apart from the sudden excesses of religious feeling, the Americans display a certain restlessness bred of anxiety about the future that robs them of pleasure they might take in their material prosperity. This too is primarily due to the Americans' attempt to find happiness through the pursuit of material things.

> A man who has set his heart on nothing but the good things of this world is always in a hurry, for he has only a limited time in which to find them, get them, and enjoy them. Remembrance of the shortness of life continually goads him on. Apart from the goods he has, he thinks of a thousand others which death will prevent him from tasting if he does not hurry. This thought fills him with distress, fear, and regret and keeps his mind continually

in agitation, so that he is always changing his plans and his abode.[27]

The Americans combat the effects of individualism in democracy and preserve a vitality for voluntary associations because the doctrine of self-interest rightly understood leads them to see the connection between self-interest and cooperation. They find the doctrine of self- interest acceptable because it fully comports with the principle of democratic equality. But the doctrine of self-interest is too narrow and simple to comprehend the entire range of emotions and passions to which men everywhere are subject. It would not, for example, suffice to explain the love of equality itself. The Americans do themselves rather less than justice in explaining that everything they do is prompted by the love of self-interest, even if qualified by the words "rightly understood." Their attempt to live down to the strictures of their own account of human motivation leads to psychological perversities—particularly unhappiness—that symptomize the partiality and artificiality of their doctrine.[28]

But the Americans *do* combat the menace of individualism. If they do not, as *they* think, learn to open their hearts to others merely by applying calculation to their greed, some other explanation is needed. In chapter 14 of Book 2, Tocqueville draws back and delivers a sweeping statement that describes what really moves the hearts of Americans. Tocqueville says in this chapter that the Americans have a love for freedom itself. It is profound, abiding, and is not derivative from anything else. Though the Americans' love of freedom is not fully intelligent or even self-conscious, it does draw them out of themselves; there is a certain boldness of spirit that will not allow an American to shut humself up within the confines of his own heart. One might recall the way that Tocqueville put it, early in Volume I: that there is a "manly and legitimate" form of the love of equality as well as a "debased taste" for it. It appears that in America the love of equality leads the weak to aspire to greatness such that it is not necessary for the strong to be dragged down to the lowest level.[29] This manly and legitimate love of equality and the love of freedom are, in fact, the same thing. There is a connection between the love of freedom and the pursuit of self-interest among the Americans, although it is not quite the connection that the Americans believe. From his own point of view, Tocqueville says that "Americans alternately display passions so strong and so similar first for their own welfare and then for liberty that one must suppose these urges to be united and mingled in some part of their being. Americans, in fact, do regard their freedom as the best tool of and the firmest guarantee for their prosperity. They love them both for the sake of each other."[30] Tocqueville goes so far as to say that this combination of the love of freedom and the love of self-interest is natural to all commercial peoples. The Tyrians, the Florentines, and the English demonstrate that commercially active nations, whether democratic or not, all tend to foster the love of freedom. (This is not to observe that to be free a nation must necessarily be commercial.) Commerce is the *activity* that puts men in contact with one another, and keeps them busy with the management of their own affairs. It gives them the occasion to feel the pleasure of freedom. Private material gain is only the nominal end for the sake of which men engage that activity; in truth they love the activity itself along with the gain that is necessarily associated with it.[31] Although the Americans are troubled by a deep restlessness and anxiety because of the way that they are consumed in commercial activity, it is because their commercial activity enables them to breathe the spirit of freedom that they can be called a great people.

Given this summary judgment of how the Americans combine the love of material well-being and the love of freedom, Tocqueville makes, in chapters 15 through 17, more expansive remarks on the subject of materialism and freedom in democracy in general that bring the central line of thought in Book 2 to a close. In chapter 15 he repeats his opposition to materialism even more strongly than he had anywhere before. Tocqueville confesses himself to be positively revolted at the pride that is displayed by those who profess materialism. "When they think they have sufficiently established that they are no better than brutes, they seem as proud as if they had proved that they were gods."[32] In this context he finally owns that the real value of any religion is that it opposes materialism by giving men a belief in the immortality of the soul.

> Most religions are only general, simple, and practical means of teaching men that the soul is immortal. That is the greatest advantage which a democratic people derives from beliefs, and it is that which makes beliefs more necessary for them than for all others.[33]

But how can religion be strong in this most important respect where materialism is strong? In chapter 16 of Book 2 Tocqueville delivers an extremely general—almost bland—speculation, but one that is important because it is directed to this question.

> There is a closer connection than is supposed between the soul's improvement and the betterment of physical conditions. A man can treat the two things as distinct and pay attention to each in turn. But he cannot entirely separate them without in the end losing sight of both.
>
> That which makes us better than the brutes in this is the way we employ our souls to find those material benefits to which instinct alone directs them. In man an angel teaches a brute how to satisfy its desires.[34]

There is then a certain kind of materialism that supports men's grasp of the divine element in their natures. That divine thing is not visible in and of itself, but it becomes visible in a way when progress towards material prosperity is taken as a *sign* of its existence. If men can come to see their material progress poetically, as pointing towards something more valuable than itself, such materialism can be a support, perhaps the best support, for spiritual life. Clearly, what Tocqueville is saying here is part of the same thought that he stated in Book I when he described the vision of the indefinite perfectibility of man as the systematic conception by which a great people governs all its affairs.[35] Rightly interpreted, indefinite progress in the direction of material prosperity can cause individuals to feel the source of greatness in their own souls. It is this that can lead them to make sacrifices—even, remarkably, to sacrifice their very lives—for a prosperity that they would rather pursue than enjoy.[36]

What Tocqueville reveals to be the connection between the soul's improvement and the betterment of physical conditions permits a summary statement about the way that self-interest is and the way that it is not at the root of the solution to the problem of democracy. The pursuit of self-interest can be either debilitating or it can be the activity through which men assume command over at least part of their own affairs, engage with their fellows, and feel the pleasure in being free. It all depends on the spirit in which it is done. But what determines the answer to *that* all important issue is another matter that remains to be formally discussed. The very purpose of Book 2, like that of Book 1, is to show that, although democracy may lead to despotism by giving men a taste for it as well as by implanting the idea in their heads, it is not necessary that it do so. The intellectual and emotional disposition of democratic citizens is *compatible* with political health, and Tocqueville shows what the signs of political health would be on the levels of opinions and feelings. But up to this point he deals only with symptoms, not with sources. The question of the spirit with which democratic citizens devote themselves to material concerns is a question of morals. Will they have the strength of soul to resist immediate gratifications and make sacrifices for the sake of longer range aims? The question of the moral strength of democratic citizens is the issue in Book 3, on the "Influence of Democracy on Mores Properly So Called." In this interpretation, Volume II has the character of an ascension; and when looked at with regard to the outline of the whole volume the main purpose of Books 1 and 2 is to point beyond their own themes towards the supreme importance of good mores, or moral strength.

The last three chapters of Book 2 deal with the theme of industrialization and "industrial aristocracy." Because these chapters are somewhat parenthetical to the rest of the book, they are likely either to be ignored or their importance to be overstressed to the detriment of the main line of argument.[37] In these chapters Tocqueville says that, although all honest callings are honorable in democracy, there is a certain preference among democratic citizens for industrial activity because the rewards tend to come more quickly than in, for example, agriculture. But industrial activity requires a high degree of specialization and hierarchy, and when that is drawn out to its limit, the social equality between laborers and management may practically disappear. "One is in a state of constant, narrow, and necessary dependence on the other and seems to have been born to obey, as the other was to command. What is this, if not an aristocracy?"[38] Tocqueville is quick to point out that this industrial aristocracy is an anomaly in democracy. It will exist only "in some industrial callings, it is an exception, a monstrosity, within the general social condition."[39] It will exist under conditions that a modern economist would call "monopsony," and the instances of that are likely to be isolated. There may develop a limited proletariat, but the rich will not withdraw into a social class with a more or less permanent membership. "To be exact, although there are rich men, a class of the rich does not exist at all, for these rich men have neither corporate spirit nor objects in common, neither common traditions nor hopes. There are limbs, then, but no body."[40] One would have to look to England, as Tocqueville describes it in his *Journey to England,* to see something like an aristocratic class that is defined by money. In that context the evil of industrialization reaches proportions from which Tocqueville can only recoil in horror. But England is herself an anomaly in this respect; *"le seul pays de la terre qui puisse donner l'idée de l'ancien régime européen, révu et perfectionné."*[41]

The narrowing of the souls of industrial laborers is not a problem of minor importance for Tocqueville, but unlike so many modern students of society, he does not think that it is *the* problem of modern society. Tocqueville considers the passion for equality rather than industrialization to be the centrally determinative fact of modern life; modern men's taste for industrial goods and their willingness to accept the conditions of work in modern industry are essentially derivative phenomena. For those who are fixated on industrialization as the mode of economic activity that fundamentally determines the form of social organization, Tocqueville's account will seem disappointingly superficial, so rooted in the terms of traditional political philosophy —"democracy," and "aristocracy"— that it misses the deeper significance of economic determinants. But unless one has recourse to Marx's understanding of the mechanics of economic determination, it is hard to see why an aristocratic class could not maintain itself indefinitely by transforming itself into an industrial aristocracy. That is, in fact, what happened in England according to Tocqueville. The fact that the history of western civilization does seem to point towards equality therefore requires another explanation than industrialization, so that industrialization itself assumes a subordinate status in the order of causes. Tocqueville can hold a realistic hope that the spread of industrialization might be checked, on the basis of an appeal to the love of equality. By pointing up the similarity between industrial organization and aristocratic social organization, Tocqueville can hope to temper modern men's natural preference (but not absolute preference) for industrial callings. In this one specific instance, Tocqueville enjoys the advantage of being allied with the spirit of democratic jealousy, and he can appeal to it directly so as to oppose this one indirect effect.

Seven

Democratic Mores: Family Life and Soldiery

The discussion in Book 3 of Volume II is directed to answering the questions that are left unanswered in Books 1 and 2. The first two books teach that democracy causes men to be receptive to the idea of despotism, and also that democracy engenders a taste for despotism. But they also teach that these effects on democratic citizens' minds and feelings are resistable, or rather alterable, so that the dead hand of despotism need not in fact result. Under the right circumstances the intellectual dispositions that Tocqueville discusses can nourish the idea of the "indefinite perfectability of man," and that idea, when acted upon, can lead a people to express their initiative and their personal resourcefulness, and thus lead to greatness. The love of equality similarly need not necessarily break down all social relationships from which men derive mutual trust and strength so as to resist the slavish need for the protection of the despot from each other. It is possible that democratic citizens will discover forms of voluntary association that will prevent them from being shut up in their own hearts, but which will not pose any serious or direct challenge to the principle of equality. The voluntary association that may exist under democracy will not be able to demand the selfless devotion for which aristocratic men prided themselves, but democratic citizens will understand their own self-interest in such a way that voluntary associations will be seen as useful to them. If Tocqueville had not been able to show how democratic beliefs and sentiments *could* be at least compatible with a non-despotical regime, he could only despair. But although he has shown why democratic opinions and sentiments do not necessarily lead to despotism, that much of the argument is not sufficient to demonstrate what will save democracy from despotism. Exhortation that aims to inspire men with the idea of their indefinite perfectability may simply fail; it *will* fail unless men actually

bear witness to the idea in their daily lives, in a robust, individualistic economy. And similarly, voluntary associations may fall victim
to the very sort of egalitarian jealousy that they are meant to resist
unless they are governed by the right spirit. All that Tocqueville
has done up to this point is describe the symptomatic forms of belief
and sentiment that will, necessarily, characterize democratic citizens
if they are to be fit for freedom.

The source of those forms of strength of mind and heart that
democratic citizens may assume is in their moral habits, or "*mores*"
as Tocqueville refers to them. This is the theme of Book 3. We need
to learn how democratic citizens may come to have the moral strength
to accept the necessary forms of authority and rank without fear
or jealousy. In giving his answer to this question Tocqueville proceeds on two different levels which may be distinguished as the
private and the public dimension of mores. The twenty-six chapters
of Book 3 are divisible into two groups, the first group of thirteen
being devoted to an exposition of democratic mores primarily within
the sphere of private societies. Tocqueville's aim here is to show that
there are democratic mores that may operate in private society,
especially in sexuality and familial relationships, that will enable
men to overcome their mutual fear and jealousy. On this level the
problem is one of resisting a kind of egalitarian idolatry that would
interfere with the natural pleasures of private relationships because
it would embarass the provisional sort of inequality that nearly all
private relations involve. Tocqueville addresses a different problem
in the remaining chapters when he turns his attention to the sort
of mores that characterize democratic citizens in the realm of public
affairs. In these last chapters he is interested in the prospects for
what we might call a public morality in democracy. The specific
problem is democracy's relative inability to satisfy the ambition of
those comparatively few people who wish to bask in the light of
their own public morality. In this latter section, Tocqueville considers how the generality of democratic citizens can be put within
reach of such public emotions by which they will rise above cynicism
and grant appropriate honor to their great men.

At least in the realm of private relationships, the source of
whatever morality democratic citizens may exhibit is a certain
gentleness, or compassion. Democratic citizens have a natural feeling for the joys and sorrows of others, and they have it because it
is easy for any of them to imagine himself in the place of another.[1]
Tocqueville's most open and even savage hostility towards aristoc-

racy as stifling compassion, which I noted in my first chapter, comes out in this context. It is here that he cites as typical of the aristocratic attitude some letters of Mme. de Sévigné. Tocqueville concludes them with the remark that Mme. de Sévigné "could not conceive clearly what it was like to suffer if one were not of noble birth."[2] Tocqueville paints a rather elaborate picture of this monster in her lace and perfume so as to appeal to our sense of moral outrage, but the bearing of his charge is much wider than even the French aristocracy of which she may have been one particularly callous member. Even the redoubtable figure of Cicero is criticized for his lack of feeling for others with whom he could not identify. Upon citing the barbarism with which the Romans treated the generals of their defeated enemies, Tocqueville says that, "Cicero, who raised such a storm of complaint about the crucifixion of a Roman citizen, had nothing to say about this atrocious abuse of victory. It is evident that in his eyes a stranger is not of the same type of humanity as a Roman."[3] In this way Tocqueville illustrates how different must be the modern, democratic forms of virtue from pre-modern forms. The ancient notion of virtue, which involved a certain resistance to sympathy or pity,[4] cannot be held up as a model any longer since that would involve a deliberate hardening of the heart against what nearly everyone feels to be the voice of goodness.

The question, then, is whether democratic citizens will in fact express their good-natured feeling for each other through acts of mutual assistance. In giving an affirmative answer to this question, Tocqueville distinguishes more carefully than he has before the differences between the consequences of democracy itself and the consequences of a democratic social revolution. He says that when men have undergone the experiences of a democratic revolution they will be much more fearful and jealous of each other than otherwise. Such men are constantly reading each other for signs of that contempt that would challenge their new and still tenuous claim to equality. But the Americans, according to Tocqueville, show that such fear need not dominate. They are not anxious about their social station, as is demonstrated by their relaxed attitude towards rules of politeness. Members of aristocratic societies require a strict regard for the rules of polite behavior because these rules are a sort of code for the expressions of deference an inferior owes to a superior and the magnanimity that a superior ought to display towards his inferiors. When, as in Europe, those relationships are blown away, men are left paralyzed because they do not know how to act. But if the Americans do not know how to act either, it does not seem to bother them; they have a healthy sort of thickheadedness that relieves them from standing, immobilized, on ceremony. It is a trait that can sometimes be inconvenient, as when one might wish to indicate to someone that his company is burdensome;[5] but that inconvenience is minor when compared to the advantage it indicates. Tocqueville pays the Americans the high compliment of saying that their manners are "simpler and more manly," supported by the "virile confidence," that each has of his own importance.[6]

The naturalness of the virtues of the Americans should not be taken to mean that they are independent of conventional support. If that were so, no practical, political science would be necessary to improve democracy. But Tocqueville shows that Americans are no different from anybody else in that their self-esteem needs to be propped up, as becomes apparent when the props are knocked out from under them. Tocqueville describes a typical American in a foreign country as becoming "so sensitive and touchy that it is hard now to avoid offending him as it once was to cause him offense."[7] Outside America, where the premise of social equality cannot be taken for granted,

> "He therefore has not the faintest notion of what status he ought to enjoy in this half-ruined hierarchy, among classes distinct enough to hate and despise each other but close enough to be always ready to get confused. He is afraid of claiming too high a status and even more afraid of being ranked too low. This double peril is a constant worry and embarrassment to his every act and word."[8]

Democratic virtues are natural, but at the same time they depend on convention, because men will not be able to express the goodness in their natures if they are anxious about their own worth, and considering the impediments to a genuine knowledge of one's worth, conventional mechanisms of support must ordinarily suffice.

Tocqueville's description of how Americans participate in private societies of various kinds suggests grounds for optimism that democratic citizens can tolerate necessary, limited sorts of inequality without feeling threatened. For example, Americans freely submit to such forms of personal service as Europeans would find degrading, without fear of being degraded. One finds a waiter performing his duties cheerfully; he shows no sign either of servility or resentment against the circumstance that has required him to take his job. The reason is that both the "master" and the "servant" in America look upon each other as equals, for whom nothing but a convenient mutuality of interest has caused a temporarily unequal station. "Why, then, has the latter the right to command, and what makes the former obey? A temporary and freely made agreement. By nature they are not at all inferior to one another, and they become so temporarily by contract. Within the terms of the contract, one is servant and the other master; beyond that, they are two citizens, two men."[9]

What Tocqueville says of the relationship between master and servant in America applies to other forms of private society as well: renter and landowner, wage laborer and capitalist, and what are clearly of most importance, husband and wife and parent and child. Tocqueville devotes a considerable space to demonstrating that democracy poses no threat to the survival or well-being of the family, although it does change the terms of familial relations. Tocqueville's discussion of these effects is central to the first part of Book 3 because it is in the family where those democratic mores that preserve the vitality of other forms of private society are to be forged.

In one sense, the difference between democratic and pre-democratic society centers on a change in the idea of the family. There is in aristocratic society a certain link between parental authority and social station. One's claim to any particular social standing is based on blood relationships. Moreover, in order for individuals to be able to inherit their social standing with a minimum of ambiguity, the rights and the authority of the father within his own family have to be held paramount. He is like a monarch over his own family; society "controls the sons through the father; it rules him, and he rules them. Hence the father has not only his natural right. He is given a political right to command."[10] Moreover, the same interest in a father's social standing being transmitted without abrogation governs the matter of his children's patrimony. The rule of primogeniture, while not absolutely necessary for aristocracy, is the norm by which such a society prevents a diffusion and recollection of property with every new generation. In America, on the other hand, the family in this "Roman and aristocratic sense" no longer exists.[11] There is a complete separation between political and familial authority, so that nothing holds the family together but temporary advantage and mutual love. In Tocqueville's view, this is a more beautiful and happier bond. The relationships among the members of an aristocratic family were necessarily more austere since the lines of social authority had to be observed within the family itself. Such austerity drives out the mutuality and intimacy of feeling that family members can be expected to have if not interfered with; this is perhaps still sensible in the bitter-sweetness of a little boy's addressing his daddy as "sir." The relations among brothers and sisters are similarly softer and more tender in democracy than in aristocracy because there is no need for any feeling of jealousy among them towards the eldest son. He is only a brother, not crown prince. In sum, Tocqueville confesses that he is "not certain, generally speaking, whether society loses by the change, but [he is] inclined to think that the individual gains."[12]

What Tocqueville says about the effect of democracy on the relations among children and parents, and among brothers and sisters, is very tempting. It constitutes a praise of democracy that goes rather far. But what has been said up to now is not the whole story. There remains the question of the effect of democracy upon the specific relationship between husband and wife, and with that the whole subject of romantic love. Is democracy compatible with the intoxicating pleasure of being overwhelmed by the image of one beloved—a passion that, so to speak, chooses us rather than one that we choose to indulge? And if such pleasure is not possible in democracy, does this not constitute a severe indictment of it, even to the point of calling into question everything that Tocqueville says in its defense? Tocqueville is keenly aware of this issue and he offers his response to it in some of the most subtle writing of his entire work. In his chapter on "The Education of Girls in the United States," Tocqueville acknowledges that there is indeed a tension between the democratic presumption that a girl ought to be the judge of her own desires and the image of her as the symbol of beauty itself, the object of a passion that reason cannot bound. The Americans educate girls to live up to the democratic presumption that each person is the judge of his own happiness, so that to find American girls charming it is necessary to bear in mind the superiority of virtue over innocence.

> Thus you can hardly expect an American girl to show that virgin innocence amid burgeoning desires and those naive and artless graces which in Europe generally go with the stage between childhood and youth. Seldom does an American girl, whatever her age, suffer from shyness or childish ignorance. She, like the Eu-

ropean girl, wants to please, but she knows exactly what it costs. She may avoid evil, but at least she knows what it is; her morals are pure rather than her mind chaste.[13]

There is, I think, a certain wry irony in these words. Tocqueville would have to expect an unbelievable sternness of heart of his reader if he thinks that we would tolerate the loss of girlish charms in return for sober virtues. Later in the same chapter, he admits that the education that is given to American girls "has its danger; [it] tends to develop judgment at the cost of imagination and to make women chaste and cold rather than tender and loving companions of men."[14] He goes so far as to say, in direct and obvious contrast to what he said of the effect of democracy on the family in general, "society may thus be more peaceful and better ordered, but the charms of private life are often less." And while he insists that "that is a secondary evil which should be faced for the sake of the greater good,"[15] one is forced to wonder—why? What greater good is there in the name of which we would sacrifice that one form of divine, albeit imaginary, pleasure that is actually within the reach of most people? If we *must* choose between justice and the charm of private life—is it not justice itself that would be rejected?

Before we jump to the conclusion that democracy necessarily destroys feminine charms and clips the wings of the heart, we need to distinguish, here as throughout the *Democracy in America*, between the effects of democracy itself and the effects of specifically American social conditions. We also need to reconsider carefully just what is meant by feminine charm. If there is a problem with American girls it is that they show no sign of ever being swept off their feet by love; they are too self-controlled to be exciting. But on the other hand, why might not a girl be the mistress of her own heart and still exciting? Can we not imagine a woman who is free and competent to give her heart as she chooses, exercising that choice just so that love will be the only criterion, and choosing the one whose love is most likely to remain pure? Can she not enter marriage willfully, just for the sake of expressing her passion for someone who will love her exclusively and without qualification?

Why, in other words, could democratic women not exhibit the qualities of "Sophy," that ideal woman whose portrait Rousseau draws to be the wife of his "Emile"? Sophy, too, is the judge of her own emotions and she chooses her husband freely. But she exercises her freedom in order to choose as her husband the man who will appreciate all her charms. I trust that the reference to Rousseau's *Emile* will not seem far fetched. I have already indicated the debt that Tocqueville owes to Rousseau in general, and with respect to Tocqueville's discussion of women, Rousseau's description seems highly pertinent. Rousseau thinks that there is no contradiction between educating women to make their own choices and teaching them the arts of charming and pleasing. It is Christianity, not women's freedom, that robs home life of its most intense pleasure. Christianity, "by exaggerating every duty, has made our duties impracticable and useless."[16] If the bonds of Christianity were relaxed though, there is no reason why women might not "cultivate the talents which will delight her husband as zealously as the Circassian cultivates the accomplishments of an Eastern harem."[17] Nor is there any reason to fear that the licensing of sexual pleasures within marriage will lead to generally licentious behavior and so weaken marriage itself. "Are not the confidence and the familiarity thus established, the innocence and the charm of the pleasures thus enjoyed, more than enough to make up for the more riotous pleasures of public entertainments?"[18] Sophy is, as the saying goes, all girl. Her charm is only enhanced by the fact she knows the nurturing that is necessary to keep the fires burning in her own heart as well as her husband's. He love empowers her even as it overpowers her.

When one looks at the American family through Tocqueville's eyes, he sees nothing of the pleasures that Rousseau describes between Emile and Sophy. But the reason that Americans approach marriage so sternly and soberly is not attributable to democracy itself, not to democratic women's self control. It derives from other factors, which Americans share with all "religious peoples and industrial nations. "In America, one sees this sternness carried to an extreme in the West. The pioneer wife lives a life of such gray duty that it is almost impossible to imagine that this woman was once a girl.

> In the utmost confines of the wilderness I have often met young wives, brought up in all the refinements of life in the towns of New England, who have passed almost without transition from their parents' prosperous houses to leaky cabins in the depths of the forest. Fever, solitude, and boredom had not broken the resilience of their courage. Their features were changed and faded, but their looks were firm. They seemed both sad and resolute.[19]

It is no wonder then that American women are not charming in the way that Sophy charms Emile. It is not because she lacks Sophy's virtues—indeed in all the fundamental respects what Tocqueville says about American women parallels almost perfectly Rousseau's description of Sophy. She knows, as does Sophy, the responsibilities she must assume in marriage. She chooses, as Sophy chooses, a man whom she believes to be himself faithful, moral, and able to provide for herself and her family. But the difference is that when she takes her vows, the American girl is steeling herself against the prospect of life-long boredom. The American girl is a Sophy who has no hope of finding a Romantic lover to be her husband.

While these reflections go a long way towards excusing American women for their lack of charm, they do not remove the cause for concern about the effects of democracy on sexuality. Tocqueville appears willing to concede that democratic marriages are likely to follow the American example rather than the beautiful example provided by Rousseau's imagination. Whereas for women to assume Sophy's virtues is hard but possible, the prospect of men's blossoming into Romantic lovers is much less likely.[20] American men are only an extreme version of the norm. So when we turn from what Rousseau shows is possible to what is actually likely, it would appear that sexuality will not provide the spice and color to human life in democracy that it did under aristocracy. Aristocratic men did not recognize the true dignity of womanhood and they did not respect its deepest charms, but precisely for that reason sexuality held the promise of delicious pleasures. Aristocracy *assumed* a tension between sexuality and morality such that sexual pleasure was a forbidden fruit—and the forbidden fruit has the sweetest taste. In his chapter on "How Equality Helps to Maintain Good Morals in America," Tocqueville explains that under aristocracy marriages often had to be arranged to serve political and social considerations. Under that condition love became something that operates outside the bonds of its legitimate place within marriage. Given that presumption, the very illegitimacy of love becomes a sort of testimony to its overweening power and to the intensity of the pleasure that it promises. All this is impossible in democracy, however, because democratic women are not under the same temptation to cheat on an agreement that they enter freely and deliberately. "For however credulous passion may make us, there is hardly a way of persuading a girl that you love her if you are perfectly free to marry her but will not do so."[21] Extending the point, Tocqueville acknowledges that because love can usually find legitimate expression in democracy it becomes less fertile a theme for poetry. Poetry makes us feel the intensity of a passion by showing us its lawlessness.[22] Small wonder that democratic husbands are such prosaic lovers.

But this comparison is on reflection not so favorable to aristocracy as it might seem if the authority of the poets were, so to speak, taken literally. Poets do not tell the whole story; they do not describe what happens to the lovers after they have broken through society's conventions.

> One should not forget that the same energy which makes a man break through a common error almost always drives him beyond what is reasonable, that to enable him to dare to declare war, even legitimately, on the ideas of his country and age means that he must have something of violence and adventure in his character, and people of this type, whatever direction they take, seldom achieve happiness or virtue. That, one may say in passing, is the reason why, even in the case of the most necessary and hallowed revolutions, one seldom finds revolutionaries who are moderate and honest.[23]

Tocqueville goes on to say that, not only are sexual affairs in aristocracy not so delicious as they are made out to be if one looks beyond the initial encounter, but moreover there is some reason to hope that democracy may eventually develop to a point where men and women might learn how to take advantage of their sexuality much more than is suggested by the example of the Americans. It is possible and, I think, appropriate to be reassured, by Tocqueville's description of the remains of the old French aristocracy, that democracy need not bring with it a prudish hostility towards sexual pleasure.

> The Revolution, which broke up the wealth of the nobles, forced them to pay attention to their affairs and to their families, compelled them to live under the same roof with their children, and finally gave a more rational and serious turn to their throughts, thereby, without their being quite conscious of this themselves, putting into their heads thoughts of respect for religious belief, love of order, quiet pleasures, and happy domestic prosperity, whereas the rest of the nation, which used naturally to have such tastes, was swept into anarchy by the sheer effort required to overthrow laws and political customs.

> One can therefore conclude, surprising though this seems at first sight, that in our day it is the most antidemocratic element in the nation which gives the best example of the moral standards one can rationally expect from democracy.[24]

Tocqueville shows by way of reference to the American family that the family must be the source of that "virile confidence" in Americans that preserves them from the sort of jealousy and anxiety that breeds despotism. Still more fundamentally, the source of the strength of the family is the virtue of American women.[25] To the extent that Tocqueville considers the delicate question of whether it is preferable for women to be virtuous or pleasing, he hints that only under a mature democracy might it be possible for them to be both.

In light of the contemporary scene, one must wonder whether Tocqueville's predictions regarding the effect of democracy on marriage, the family, and sexuality are not perhaps the most significant failing of his thought. He seems, unhappily, out of focus in his confidence that democracy poses no real threat to the sanctity and strength of marriage. One must wonder whether, if he were alive today, he could still maintain that democracy does not undermine society's recognition of a difference in the roles that should be performed by the two sexes. For him, there is no problem in thinking that women might be granted equality with men in the fundamental respect of having an equal right at birth to liberty, and at the same time thinking that men and women will continue to assume different familial and therefore social responsibilities. He thinks "it is easy to see that the sort of equality [that some Europeans would force] on both sexes degrades them both, and that so coarse a jumble of nature's words could produce nothing but feeble men and unseemly women."[26] Tocqueville thinks rather that the Americans exemplify the attitude that will typify a mature democracy regarding the differentiation between the sexes.

> They think that nature, which created such great differences between the physical and moral constitution of men and women, clearly intended to give their diverse faculties a diverse employment; and they consider that progress consists not in making dissimilar creatures do roughly the same things but in giving both a chance to do their job as well as possible. The Americans have applied to the sexes the great principle of political economy which now dominates industry.[27]

Tocqueville's confidence that his endorsement will be followed is based on the expectation that people will choose to perform sexual roles because they are convenient, in a rather full sense of that word, even when they are no longer necessary to each individual's station in a social hierarchy. And when we consider the sweetness of a loving union between a man and a woman each performing a distinct role that complements rather than competes with the other, that expectation does seem plausible. But has Tocqueville correctly identified and gauged the hostility towards sexual role identification as a constraint upon one's freedom to pursue happiness on one's own terms? Tocqueville was, of course, not unaware that under some circumstances democracy had brought about a rejection of the idea of distinct roles for men and women in the family and in society, together with a certain strident form of sexual license. But when he writes of this, he explains it by appealing to his distinction between "revolutionary" habits and those which are truly democratic, and he supports his point by way of reference to the sexual mores in America, where the Revolution never needed to happen.[28] This obviously hopeful interpretation of the significance of American mores turns on his dismissal of the traditional notion, as in Plato's *Republic*, for example, that the soul has at its core a tyrannical lust that seeks to overcome all restraints in law and decency as reminding it of its mortal condition.[29] To pursue this point would require going beyond Tocqueville's writing, to consider Rousseau's *Emile*, where he joins Plato directly.[30] As far as *Democracy in America* goes, we are simply left to wonder whether it really is true that men and women will live up to the requirements of marriage and family because they can feel the convenience and the charm of those things.

In chapters 14 through 26 of Book 3 Tocqueville moves on a different plane from that of the first thirteen chapters. Here he considers democratic mores in the sphere of public life, and his specific subjects include ambition and honor, and also war. The central problem in this section is that posed by ambition for public recognition or honor; the problem that receives its most succinct formulation in the famous and difficult eighteenth chapter of Book 3. What place, if any, can an ambitious man have in democracy?

The four chapters that precede chapter 18 provide an introduction to the formulative statement regarding ambition and honor that comes in chapter 18. In this context Tocqueville first observes that the manners of democratic citizens, in the sense of standards of politeness, are very crude. In a way it is true that democratic citizens have no manners at all.[31] The reason for this is that "true dignity in manners consists in always taking one's proper place, not too high and not too low";[32] but in democracy no one knows his place. Tocqueville's comment on the unmannered behavior of the Americans is oddly wistful. He is not certain whether in the ultimate scale of things politeness is very important, but he confesses his own well-mannered taste with the remark that "one should not attach too much importance to this loss, but it is permissible to regret it."[33] Tocqueville then goes on to explain his ambivalence towards the decay in manners in democracy by reflecting on the relationship between manners and genuine virtue. "Though the manners of an aristocracy by no means create virtue, they may add grace to virtue itself."[34] A dignified manner suggests that one is above petty concerns; he can afford to be concerned with virtue for its own sake. Moreover, while it is possible for men to appreciate even the full value of virtue without assuming a lofty and dignified bearing, such men would be denied a certain form of pleasure that at one time had distinguished those who cared for virtue. It is then as if democracy required us to enjoy food without flavor; and although Tocqueville insists that it is not legitimate or rational to react with indignant violence to that requirement, he recognizes that it would be inhuman not to feel what has been lost.

As his discussion proceeds, Tocqueville steadily draws his reader to feel the severity of the problem indicated above. While in chapter 14 Tocqueville permits us a certain nostalgia for the courtly behavior of aristocratic society, in the subsequent chapters he draws out those features of the American character that make questionable our ability to maintain our own self-esteem in an aristocracy. Some of Tocqueville's most uncomplimentary remarks about the Americans occur in this context. For example, he says that despite their sternness, the Americans are not really a serious minded people. One can hear the wildest half-baked notions expressed in public. No one, it seems, ever stands to lose his reputation among democratic citizens for suggesting in public a crazy idea.[35] Another observation along this same line is that the Americans are quarrelsome out of restlessness.[36] The general equality of social condition makes the slightest advantage tell, and at the same time makes those advantages precarious, so that the democratic citizen is in a condition of "constant alarm and anxiety."[37] But among such boors, who have no sense of propriety in speech or gesture, and whose anger is quick and shallow, how is it possible to retain one's own composure?

While we could smile tolerantly with Tocqueville at democracy's bad manners, these additional defects of character move us to contempt and anger; and we are not so comfortably removed from the thing that angers us. Chapters 15 through 17 describe a society that looks like a nest of hornets, and in it there is no place for the man who would stand "unmoved in solitary grandeur."[38] Unless one were simply above all feelings of anger, how could he avoid being dragged down into democracy's monotonous, nasty buzz?

The culmination of these concerns is chapter 18, "Concerning Honor in the United States and Democratic Societies." Tocqueville opens this chapter with some broad observations that will be familiar to students of Montesquieu. He says that honor can mean either the glory or esteem that men seek to win, or the rules by which they seek to win it.*[39] Honor in the second sense was bred by medieval institutions as a result of the particular requirements of that society. Valor in war and fidelity to one's liege were the principal characteristics of an honorable man.[40] Tocqueville goes on to distinguish medieval honor from the corresponding phenomenon in the ancient cities—i.e., virtue. Virtue is like honor in that certain rules of behavior come to be valued because they serve the needs of a particular society, but the difference is that, while medieval honor involves a devotion to some person, virtue involves devotion to the community itself. In the medieval context, what is considered honorable behavior depends upon the particular person towards whom the behavior is directed and the person who is performing the action, whereas the ancient idea of political virtue comes closer to being a generic term, at least within the confines of one city.[41] Among fellow citizens, virtue means one thing. In this context, Tocqueville says that Americans too have a notion of virtue, parallel to the ancient notion. The habits useful in trade and industry have become the virtues of American citizens.[42]

---

*This double meaning of the word indicates the curious thing about honor that Tocqueville recognizes. The question might be asked, which of the two senses of the term "honor" is the primary one? That is, does the man of honor wish to be honored and does he obey the rules of honor for that reason, or does he wish to deserve honor such that he would obey its rules even if his doing so went unnoticed? The answer that has to be given is, "both." He wishes to be deservedly honored. But honor, then, involves a concession to the importance of public recognition, and to the authority of public opinion, that marks its own infirmity—and democracy threatens to blow the cover that shields and preserves the honorable man.

Having followed Montesquieu's lead almost perfectly thus far, Tocqueville then blurs the distinction between honor and virtue, using the terms almost interchangeably and highlighting the word "honor." He reveals that what is important for his purpose is the similarity between honor and virtue. The critical thing is that both are in their own way particularistic.[43] By emphasizing this common feature of virtue and honor he is able to treat virtue as a form of honor, for, in truth, "that which our ancestors called, par excellence, honor, was really only one of its forms."[44] He sets up a continuum, with medieval society at one end where the rules of honor were very strict and complex, and democratic society at the other where what honor prescribes is less precise and less demanding.[45] On this continuum the classical cities fall somewhere in between the extremes. Tocqueville's point is that the prescriptiveness of the rules of honor is measured by the degree of peculiarity and distinctiveness of the social requirements that it serves. Since "there is always something much more peculiar about the position of a caste than about that of a nation," the rules of honor that mark off and support a caste are the strictest.[46]

Having presented this reformulation of Montesquieu's idea in broad outline, Tocqueville then draws his conclusion—a conclusion which he says "has never been clearly pointed out before."[47] As equality of conditions becomes more and more the rule, "all the peculiar notions which each class styled honor begin successively to disappear."[48] Ultimately, only the nations themselves remain as a source of distinctions among mankind, and "honor stands for the peculiar individual character of that nation before the world."[49] Even this is not the end of the matter. The movement towards democracy is not confined to one nation; it is possible to imagine, or rather impossible not to imagine, that at some point even nations and races would lose their distinctive features. Under *that* condition the implications of Tocqueville's vision are that "the practice of attributing a conventional value to men's actions would cease altogether. Everyone would see them in the same light. The general needs of humanity, revealed to each man by his conscience, would form the common standard."[50] Tocqueville concludes chapter 18 with the sweeping statement that "it is the dissimilarities and inequalities among men which give rise to the notion of honor; as such differences become less, it grows feeble; and when they disappear, it will vanish too."[51]

It is important to note in the conclusion of chapter 18 that Tocqueville does not exactly predict that democracy will lead to a breaking down of nationhood, bringing about a universal, homogeneous society. What he says is that "if one can *suppose*"[52] such a thing, it would mean the end of the idea of honor. Democracy invites that very supposition. Tocqueville has said that America, for example, *does* have its distinctive notions of what constitutes honorable behavior, and that those notions derive from the requirements of trade and commerce. But, especially in the context of Tocqueville's earlier remarks on poetry in democracy, there is a certain universalism implicit in the way that democracy conducts its commerce. The poetic vision of the Americans points beyond the existence of the American nation towards a "vast democracy in which each nation counts as a single citizen."[53] With reference to the lesson in chapter 18 we can say that the conventional notions of honor among the Americans point to their own conventionality.

The importance of this observation can be seen in connection with what Tocqueville says in the sequel to chapter 18. In these latter chapters of Book 3, Tocqueville is concerned with the specific problem posed by ambition in democracy. Ambition means an overweening desire for honor above all else. If it were the case that the actual future of the world offered no satisfaction for the ambitious desire for honor, Tocqueville would be forced to conclude simply that ambition is a sort of criminal disease in the world of the future, and it should be bottled up or else exterminated; but this is decidedly not his view. On the contrary, he confesses that

> what frightens me most is the danger that, amid all the constant trivial preoccupations of private life, ambition may lose both its force and its greatness, that human passions may grow gentler and at the same time baser, with the result that the progress of the body social may become daily quieter and less aspiring. I therefore think that the leaders of the new societies would do wrong if they tried to send the citizens to sleep in a state of happiness too uniform and peaceful, but that they should sometimes give them difficult and dangerous problems to face, to rouse ambition and give it a field of action.[54]

It is important not to read chapter 18 as actually predicting a future where there is no prospect for the satisfaction of honor. A more precise reading questions how men can seek to win honor within conventional standards that they know to be merely conventional standards. Put this way, the question is not so troublesome for the generality of men, because most people do seem to conform to conventional standards almost instinctively, even though they have a kind of awareness that their values or standards are conventional, so long as those conventions are consistent with their convenience. But Tocqueville's discussion in the latter chapters of Book 3 leaves most people to one side. He is specifically concerned with those who desire honor itself above all else, as distinct from those for whom it is enough that no burden of dishonor interfere with their pursuit of material gain. The ambitious man does not want honor to be convenient. He wishes inconvenience, so better to demonstrate his deservedness. What can democracy hold for him?

As Tocqueville's discussion of the problem of the ambitious man in democracy proceeds, it becomes clearer that what makes his situation so frustrating is not so much his own jaundiced view of his society's conventions, as it is the casual attitude of the generality of the people towards what must be the terms of his own honor. From the perspective of the ambitious man, the people appear lethargic; they seem not to feel the hunger that drives him, and they have no appreciation of the virtue he would like to exhibit. Tocqueville develops this point in chapter 21, "Why Great Revolutions Will Become Rare." Near the opening of this chapter Tocqueville issues the warning that this "subject is important, and I ask the reader to follow my argument closely."[55] The central point of this chapter is that, contrary to the opinion Tocqueville attributes to many of his contemporaries, democracy is not an unstable and revolutionary condition. The great class of men in democracy who are owners of modest amounts of property are the natural enemies of violent conditions: "Their excitement about small matters makes them calm about great ones."[56] The consequence of what Tocqueville asserts here is that there is a disjunction that robs the ambitious few of a field of expression.

> I am not suggesting that they resist him openly by means of well-thought-out schemes, or indeed by means of any considered determination to resist. They show no energy in fighting him and sometimes even applaud him, but they do not follow him. Secretly their apathy is opposed to his fire, their conservative interests to his revolutionary instincts, their homely taste to his adventurous passion, their common sense to his flighty genius, their prose to his poetry. With immense effort he rouses them for a moment, but

they soon slip from him and fall back, as it were, by their own weight. He exhausts himself trying to animate this indifferent and preoccupied crowd and finds at last that he is reduced to impotence, not because he is conquered but because he is alone.[57]

Though democracy is not incapable of being inspired by thoughts of public glory, it is hard to get equal men to *sacrifice* much for it. The ambitious are frustrated and become the enemies of society. Given *this* restatement of the issue, what is principally required in order to civilize extraordinary ambition is that the generality of men somehow be rendered fit to recognize and appreciate the value of such ambition. They must not be allowed to remain wholly preoccupied with their private activity; they must rather be put within reach of "those great and powerful public emotions which do indeed perturb peoples but which also make them grow and refresh them."[58] With regard to this special problem of the role of the ambitious in democracy, we must conclude that the vision of the nation's glory that is conveniently conducive to the general pursuit of private satisfaction is *not* sufficient. The commercial glory of the democratic nation is an image that satisfies only the more modest form of political passion. It yields a sense of honor satisfactory only to those who are not driven by a yearning for honor above all else. A people that is fit to reward with appropriate honors the actions of those who are driven most by ambition must themselves enter the field of those "great and powerful public emotions" that drive men to the greatest heights. Having made this point, Tocqueville abruptly and without further explanation turns to the subject of the last five chapters of Book 3—the prospects for war in democracy and for democracy in war.

The most dangerous form of the danger to democracy from its most ambitious element is war. "All those who seek to destroy the freedom of the democratic nations must know that war is the surest and shortest means to accomplish this. That is the very first axiom of their science."[59] Just as Tocqueville does not think that the problem of ambition can be resolved by purging democracy of its ambitious men, so Tocqueville does not think that democracy can purge itself of war and the concern with war. War would not be impossible unless there ceased to be distinct nations: a situation that is equivalent to the triumph of the worst prospects in democracy. For this reason Tocqueville takes it for granted that "war is a hazard to which all nations are subject, democracies as well as the rest."[60] The question is, how can the threat of war be *minimized* in conformity with the conditions necessary to the highest and strongest expression of public emotion?

Having said that all nations are necessarily subject to the hazard of war, Tocqueville says that war is not an unqualified evil. All too easily understressed is his statement that

> I do not wish to speak ill of war; war almost always widens a nation's mental horizons and raises its heart. In some cases it may be the only factor which can prevent the exaggerated growth of certain inclinations naturally produced by equality and be the antidote needed for certain inveterate diseases to which democratic societies are liable.[61]

In keeping with the central issue that underlies the last several chapters of Book 3, Volume II, the significance of this qualified praise of war is that the only way that a people can be brought within reach of those truly "great and powerful emotions" is to involve them in thinking about war. A people that is fit to bestow with appropriate honors those who are most ambitious for honor must themselves know the nobility of the ultimate sacrifice a citizen can make for his country. The reader whose sympathy Tocqueville has won up to this point will have been prepared to draw the conclusion for himself, and Tocqueville, understandably, stops short of making it explicit. The people who are fit to honor their best citizens must combine the role of citizen and soldier, perhaps through the institution of universal military service.

The problem of reconciling nobility and democracy, which is *the* problem of democracy from Tocqueville's point of view, absolutely requires a combination of the roles; of democratic citizen and soldier. This fact surely does not mean that Tocqueville recommends war and conquest as a way of life for modern democratic nations. But, like Machiavelli,[62] Tocqueville suggests that a free people must never believe that their freedom depends on any security other than their own military strength. A citizenry that is disarmed and puts its trust in hirelings (Tocqueville's example here is the non-commissioned officer —the professional soldier) runs an *increased risk of war*; and moreover, it runs an increased risk of *defeat*. As Tocqueville describes him, the professional is susceptible to a reckless kind of ambition for war. War is the only condition in which rapid promotion is possible; therefore the professional soldier "wants

war; he always wants it and at any cost."[63] Tocqueville would prevent
the spirit of the professional soldier from characterizing the democratic army because he wants to civilize soldiery as well as to en-
noble citizenship. The remedy for the army's vices can only be
sought in the pacific and orderly habits of the private, citizen soldier.[64]

One question remains of Tocqueville's discussion of war and
democracy. Is the citizen army that Tocqueville seems to be recommending really fit to fight and win in a contest with trained
professionals? Tocqueville considers this question in some detail,
with the conclusion that democratic citizens *can* make excellent soldiers. There is, he notes, an often hidden connection between the
spirit of democracy and the war passion.

> Moreover, there is a hidden connection which war uncovers be-
> tween the military and democratic mores.
>
> The men of democracies are by nature passionately eager to
> acquire quickly what they covet and to enjoy it on easy terms.
> They for the most part love hazards and fear death much less
> than difficulty. It is in that spirit that they conduct their trade
> and industry, and this spirit carried with them onto the battlefield
> induces them willingly to risk their lives to secure in a moment
> the rewards of victory. No kind of greatness is more pleasing to
> the imagination of a democratic people than military greatness
> which is brilliant and sudden, won without hard work, by risking
> nothing but one's life.
>
> An aristocratic people which, fighting against a democracy, does
> not succeed in bringing it to ruin in the first campaigns always
> runs a great risk in being defeated by it.[65]

Tocqueville goes still beyond this statement in accounting for
the excellence of the democratic army. Democracy's greatest advantage in war is that it is well constituted to recognize the glory
that its citizens may win in battle. Aristocracy, by contrast, has
difficulty seeing that it is a man's *own* life that he risks for his
country.

> The [aristocratic] soldier has broken into military discipline, so
> to say, before he enters the army, or rather military discipline is
> only a more perfect form of social servitude. So in aristocratic
> armies the private soon comes to be insensible to everything
> except the orders of the leaders. He acts without thought, triumphs
> without excitement, and is killed without complaint. In such a

condition he is no more a man, but he is a very formidable animal trained for war.[66]

Democracy, however, is freer with its gratitude. Indeed, Tocqueville's discussion of the military advantages of democracy reads like a straightforward elaboration of what Machiavelli says regarding the vital differences between the people and the nobles—that the nobles are stingy with their gratitude.[67]

Marshall Rommel is alleged to have said on some occasion that the soldiers of the American democratic army are the fiercest and hence the best that he opposed—after the first battle. Whether Rommel actually said that tribute or not it nicely accords with what Tocqueville reveals as the root of democracy's natural supremacy. Democracy fights only at first with instruments, but afterwards with men. Tocqueville's discussion of war and democracy reveals that what he means by the noble love of equality is in fact the warrior spirit. His central purpose in *Democracy in America* can be summed up as an attempt to keep that spirit alive.

> Democratic peoples must despair of ever obtaining from their soldiers this blind, detailed, resigned, and equable obedience which aristocracies can impose without trouble. The state of society in no way prepares men for this, and there is a danger that they will lose their natural advantages by trying artificially to acquire this one. In democracies military discipline ought not to try to cancel out the spontaneous exercise of the faculties; it should aspire only to direct them; and the obedience thus trained will be less precise but more impetuous and intelligent. It should be rooted in the will of the man who obeys; it relies not only on instinct, but on reason too, and consequently will often grow stricter as the danger makes this necessary. The discipline of an aristocratic army is apt to relax in wartime, for it is based on habit, and war upsets habits. But in a democratic army discipline is strengthened in the face of the enemy, for each soldier sees very clearly that to conquer he must be silent and obey.
>
> Those nations that have achieved most in war have never known any other discipline than that of which I speak. In antiquity only free men and citizens were accepted for the army, and they differed but little from one another and were accustomed to treat one another as equals. In that sense the armies of antiquity can be called democratic, even when they sprang from an aristocratic society. As a result, in those armies a sort of fraternal familiarity

prevailed between officers and men. To read Plutarch's lives of great commanders convinces one of that. The soldiers are constantly talking, and talking very freely, to their generals, while the latter gladly listen to what they say and answer it. Their words and their example lead the army much more than any constraint or punishment. They were as much companions as leaders to their men.

I do not know if the Greeks and Romans ever brought the small details of military discipline to such perfection as the Russians have done, but that did not prevent Alexander from conquering Asia, and the Romans the world.[68]

Tocqueville believes himself to be under the necessity imposed by the revelation of the idea of humanity to show how that idea can lead men to aspire to greatness rather than to sink down to a sort of atomism animated by jealousy and presided over by a new form of despotism. He intends to show that such an aspiration to greatness requires the development of a social ritual by which the equal right of all at birth to liberty can be given active, political expression, in the manner of Rousseau's general will. In general, he has tried to show how, rightly interpreted, commerce can be that activity through which the general will feels itself existent. But in the final analysis commerce is only a second best approximation of *the* ritual that makes a moral whole of a body of individuals. The political virtue, the "species of heroism," that commerce illuminates is but an allusion to the more authentic species of heroism in war. The idea of self-sacrifice that commerce *can* point towards is only a simile to the self-sacrifice of the citizen soldier. The freedom, in the sense of the word Tocqueville intends to convey when he describes the New England Puritans in the early part of Volume I, has its most obvious example, and in a way its best example, in the democratic soldier who served with Alexander.

Eight

Conclusion

The fourth book of Volume II of *Democracy in America* is Tocqueville's own conclusive summary of the work. Since it would be for the most part repetitious to extend my interpretation to this summary, I will instead conclude my study with a broad comment on what I think to be the value of reading Tocqueville today.

Tocqueville's "new science of politics" is intended to be both prescriptive as well as descriptive.[1] His descriptions are in the service of what he prescribes. His overall aim is to preserve liberty against the danger of dead level equality brought about by democratic jealousy. That jealousy is one of the two forms of the love of equality, and while the love of equality cannot be resisted in any way, it can be affected so that it expresses itself nobly and not jealously. The fundamental distinction for the entire work is the one drawn early in Volume I between, "a manly and legitimate passion for equality which rouses in all men a desire to be strong and respected (and which) tends to elevate the little man to the rank of the great . . . [and] a debased taste for equality, which leads the weak to want to drag the strong down to their level and which induces men to prefer equality in servitude in inequality in freedom."[2] Tocqueville thinks that the nobler love of equality requires putting democratic citizens within reach of those great public emotions by which a people feels its own existence. Democracy needs to be helped to appreciate its own grandeur. Tocqueville actually does think that there is a species of grandeur that is natural to democracy. It is a grandeur that is more individualistic, more consistent with self-improvement, even more mundane than the grandeur of the *ancien régime*, but it is also something that can inspire the poetic imagination of a people.

Although Tocqueville is explicit about his intention that his reader find useful lessons from his study, the prescriptions that he gives are unspecific and oblique. He presents his practical lessons always by example, but the example is American democracy, and for reasons that are fairly clear, America cannot be imitated. In order to ferret out Tocqueville's teaching it is necessary to distinguish American from democratic things and then to use our imagination to decide how American institutions would have to be modified to suit different circumstances. This turns out to be no small task, for the degree of the uniqueness of the American situation means that the modification would have to be significant. The fact that America has no anti-democratic history, and also the boundlessness of the American continent, are the fortunate circumstances whereby America shows that democratic society *can* enjoy the advantages of decentralization, local self-government, and a respect for the rights of property. The democratic jealousy, which is *the* problem for most democracies, is not so dangerous in America because of the field for the expression of sub- political passion, and the lack of even the memory of a common enemy. Curiously then, the very reason for which America can illustrate so nicely the essential character of democracy and the advantages it can have is also the reason why America cannot exhibit the measures and mechanisms by which those advantages can be secured under more ordinary circumstances. What America has achieved by luck, European statesmen must try to accomplish by art. European statesmen will have to confront squarely and redirect the democratic passion for equality—Tocqueville remains tantalizingly silent as to just how that might be done.

Still, we can draw some rather general inferences as to how European democracies should be governed. In contrast to the United States, European governments will have to be more centralized. They will have to be able to make a more direct appeal to public emotion, and they will have to be organized to perform great deeds. At the same time provincial liberties should be preserved and the people required to take as active a part in the administration of their own affairs as possible. Both these considerations require that the government be strongly executive in character. Tocqueville marvelled, but with foreboding, at the ability of the Americans to submit themselves to the election of their chief executive every four years; he doubted whether France would survive such shocks.[3] Years later, in his *Recollections* on the "revolution" of 1848, Tocqueville confessed that he

> did not believe ... that the republican form of government is best suited to the needs of France. What I mean when I say the

republican form of government, is the Executive Power. With a people among whom habit, tradition, custom have assured so great a place to the Executive Power, its instability will always be, in periods of great excitement, a cause of revolution, and in peaceful times, a cause of great uneasiness. Moreover, I have always considered the Republic an ill balanced form of government which always promised more, but gave less, liberty than the Constitutional Monarchy.[4]

Tocqueville's belief in the utility of Constitutional Monarchy, and its compatibility with democratic instincts, is an important feature of his thought, and I think it deserves special attention today. This is not to say that the formula, "Constitutional Monarchy" is the final piece of the puzzle by which Tocqueville's practical teaching becomes clear. Much depends on the personality of the constitutional monarch. Tocqueville supported the regime of Louis Phillipe, not because it embodied his hopes for a democratic regime that would enoble the democratic passion and provide a field for the "manly" love of equality. The July Monarchy, like the short-lived Republic that followed it, were thought by Tocqueville to be patched-up affairs, which he supported as temporizing measures lest France be dragged down by the petty egalitarianism of the Jacobins.[5] But beyond such measures, there is in Tocqueville a call for a certain kind of leadership—for a leader of the appropriate character and personality who might, as Tocqueville says of the great Bonaparte, "fill the immense stage that the Revolution had opened." Tocqueville cannot produce such a person. At best his work might be of some guidance should one come along. He would have to have his own ability to seize his own opportunity among his own people.

The source of Tocqueville's perceptiveness and his ingenuity is his grasp of the relation between freedom and equality. The most serious questions are also raised at this point. Fundamentally, men are equal on the level of their birthright to freedom. Democracy is distinctive because it acknowledges this fact, whereas the *ancien régime* understood freedom only as a privilege. But freedom is a mystery and so the true ground of human equality eludes our recognition. Perhaps, ultimately, only God himself can know it, by virtue of his ability to take in the entire human race in one glance, and see each one individually. Since human beings are not able to do that, we necessarily have recourse to generalities and abstractions. The danger in this is that freedom itself may become an abstraction, and as such it is something in the name of which the new form of despotism spreads its influence.

Given this situation, Tocqueville thinks that modern men need to be brought to *feel* the charms of self-reliance, voluntary co-operation and ultimately, self-government. Tocqueville counts on the real pleasure arising from the active expression of freedom to resist the new despotism. But when the elaborate account of how such active freedom is compatible with self-interest and the love of equality is finally sorted out, one still wonders whether Tocqueville has not confused the signs of political health with the cause. Can the idea of freedom, which is Tocqueville's own supreme standard, animate a people's common life? "The general will must act," says Rousseau, speaking to the same issue, but what action could the idea of freedom recommend? Revolution perhaps, but what then? Rousseau recommends that Montesquieu be examined for an answer to the question of what forms a people's common life, and Tocqueville follows that lead. Still, one wonders whether the concession to the significance of specific circumstances that Montesquieu had illuminated is not a way that Tocqueville dodges the hard question. The particular circumstances of a nation do have their effect on the form of common life—as constraints. The question for Tocqueville though, is not how to constrain a people, but rather how to move them.

The ultimate reason for the intriguing, arresting, even baffling character of *Democracy in America* is its Rousseauan foundation. When Tocqueville asserts the desirability of democratic citizens' being put within reach of great and powerful public emotions, he is asserting the need for the general will to be conscious of itself. As Rousseau taught, however, the general will is essentially contentless; it is a sort of enlarged version of the riddling character of the human soul as a sentiment of its own existence. Tocqueville appears to write from the premise that the democratic legislator will be able to respond intelligently to the infinitely varied circumstances of political life only if he understands this fundamental riddle of democracy's soul; and to be properly learned, the lesson needs to be conveyed by way of an elaboration of practical example. At the same time, as he makes it possible for us to penetrate his discussion of the example of democracy in America, Tocqueville cannot help but bring us to question the desirability of democracy itself.

Notes

Chapter One

1. Alexis de Tocqueville, *Democracy in America*, ed. J. P. Mayer and Max Lerner, trans. George Lawrence (New York: Harper and Row, 1966), p. 6.

2. Jack Lively notes that, "From the very first, he was hailed by every shade of political opinion as its exponent and defender." Jack Lively, *Social and Political Thought of Alexis de Tocqueville* (Oxford: Clarendon Press, 1962), p. 7.

3. An example is Robert Nisbet, *Twilight of Authority* (New York: Oxford University Press, 1975), esp. pp. 273–4. The reader may wish to compare Nisbet's judgement of the relationship between Tocqueville and Rousseau, which differs from mine. cf. Nisbet, *Twilight of Authority*, pp. 196, 208–9.

4. Raymond Aron, *Main Currents in Sociological Thought*, trans. Richard Howard and Helen Weaver (New York: Basic Books, Inc., 1965).

5. Marvin Zetterbaum, *Tocqueville and the Problem of Democracy* (Stanford: Stanford University Press, 1967).

6. Lively, *Social and Political Thought*.

7. Seymour Drescher, *Tocqueville and England* (Cambridge: Harvard University Press, 1964).

8. Aron, *Main Currents*, p. 204.

9. Tocqueville, *Democracy in America*, pp. 3–6.

10. The distinctiveness of Tocqueville's answer to this question is, I think, commonly overlooked because contemporary social scientists tend not to see the seriousness of the question. That is, we tend to assume a quasi-Marxism insofar as we take historical progress towards equality to be normal. It takes an effort to resist that tendency. I think a good example of this is provided by Samuel Beer in his text on comparative government. Beer says that what generated democracy was scientific rationalism plus "voluntarism," i.e. the idea that the legitimacy of a public policy or a regime derives from mere human wishes as distinct from the medieval notion of an objective scale of values that some might know better than others. "There is in voluntarism a certain openness that readily becomes a tendency toward democracy. Perhaps the reason is simply that although it is hard to deny

149

that knowledge of the good . . . is unevenly distributed throughout society, it is self-evident that every man has wants to satisfy." Thus, democracy is the outcome of the exposure that the aristocratic class does not have a clear grasp of values by which their rule might be defended. But would an aristocrat imagine that he would ever be able to *demonstrate* the values that make his rule legitimate? Would it ever occur to him to make the attempt? I find it easy to attribute to the *aristocratic* man a rather far reaching "voluntaristic," or subjectivistic attitude; I imagine him thinking that as he wishes to rule there are many among his social inferiors who would like to displace him. But why would he accord those wishes *any* value in comparison with his own? Authority is the prerogative of majesty, which he enjoys, and the inferiors only envy and adore. What need is there for an objective value by which some disinterested party might prefer the aristocrat's wishes? Something still further is necessary in order to explain why the mere fact that the other man has wishes too raises a question about the primacy of one's own. I think that Tocqueville addresses himself to this dimension of the issue. cf. Samuel H. Beer, et al., *Patterns of Government*, (New York: Random House, 1973), esp. p. 60.

11. Tocqueville, *Democracy in America*, pp. 5–6.

12. Ibid., p. 5.

13. Ibid., p. 404.

14. Ibid., p. 538.

15. Aristotle, *Politics*, ed. and trans. E. Barker (New York: Oxford University Press, 1962), bk. III, chap. VII.

16. Tocqueville, *Democracy in America*, p. 517.

17. Ibid., p. 539.

18. Ibid., p. 518.

19. Richard Herr, *Tocqueville and the Old Regime* (Princeton: Princeton University Press, 1962), p. 48, n. 9.

20. *See* Carl J. Friedrich, Introduction, *The Philosophy of Kant*, ed. and trans. Carl J. Friedrich (New York: The Modern Library, 1949), pp. xxii–xxiii.

21. Immanuel Kant, "Metaphysical Foundations of Morals," in *The Philosophy of Kant*, ed. and trans. Carl J. Friedrich (New York: The Modern Library, 1949).

22. Ibid., p. 178.

23. J. J. Rousseau, *The Social Contract*, trans. Willmoore Kendall (Chicago: Henry Regnery Company, 1954), p. 61.

24. Alexis de Tocqueville, *The European Revolution and Correspondence with Gobineau*, ed. and trans. John Lukacs (Garden City: Doubleday and Company, Inc., 1959), esp. letter # XII, November 17, 1853, pp. 226–30.

25. Tocqueville, *Democracy in America*, p. 7.

26. Ibid., p. 8.

27. Ibid., p. 9.

28. Ibid., p. 11.

29. Ibid., p. 10.

30. Ibid.

31. Ibid., p. 11.

32. Ibid., p. 12.

33. Ibid., p. 11.

34. Ibid., p. 12.

35. Zetterbaum records this view, approvingly. Zetterbaum, *Problem of Democracy*, p. 40.

36. Tocqueville, *Democracy in America*, p. 584.

37. Aristotle, *Politics*, pp. 133–6.

38. Tocqueville, *Democracy in America*, p. 643.

39. Ibid., p. 13.

40. Alexis de Tocqueville, *Ancien Regime*, trans. Stuart Gilbert (Garden City: Doubleday and Co., 1955), p. 169.

Chapter Two

1. J. P. Mayer cites Sainte-Beuve's opinion to this effect in his introduction to the text of *Democracy in America*, pp. xii–iii.

2. Tocqueville, *Democracy in America*, pp. 153, 154–5.

3. Ibid., p. 24.

4. Ibid., p. 27.

5. Ibid., pp. 21–2.

6. Ibid., p. 22.

7. The subsequent discussion of the Indians is in the tenth and last chapter of Part II, Volume I.

8. The obvious reference is to Rousseau's *Discourse on the Origin of Inequality*. The specific point mentioned here can also be found in the first book of the *Social Contract* wherein Rousseau says that to enter civil society one must abandon every one of his natural rights, but in so doing one is able to enjoy a civil freedom that leaves one as free as before—but not in the same way. Rousseau, *The Social Contract*, trans. Willmoore Kendall (Chicago: Henry Regnery Company, 1954), pp. 18–19.

9. Tocqueville, *Democracy in America*, p. 26.

10. Ibid., p. 29.

11. Ibid., p. 30.

12. Ibid., p. 34.

13. Ibid., pp. 34–5.

14. Ibid., p. 36.

15. Ibid., pp. 36, 38.

16. Ibid., pp. 47–9.

17. Ibid., p. 45.

18. Ibid.

19. Ibid., p. 49.

20. Ibid., p. 53.

21. Ibid., p. 55.

22. Ibid., pp. 55–6.

23. Ibid., p. 57. Compare Rousseau's *Social Contract* where he says that the people must govern themselves directly and not through representatives if there is to be a general will. Rousseau, *Social Contract*, pp. 140–153.

24. Ibid., p. 103.

25. Ibid., p. 140.

26. Ibid., p. 59.

27. Ibid., pp. 83–5.

28. Ibid., p. 78.

29. Ibid., p. 81.
30. Ibid., p. 361.
31. Ibid., p. 67.
32. Ibid., pp. 70–1.
33. Ibid., p. 71.
34. Ibid., pp. 80–81, 149–50.
35. Ibid., pp. 89–93.
36. Ibid., p. 92.
37. Ibid., p. 94.
38. Ibid., p. 96.
39. Ibid., p. 100.
40. Ibid., p. 153.
41. Ibid., p. 151.
42. Ibid., pp. 153, 154.
43. Ibid., p. 361.
44. Ibid., p. 104.
45. Ibid., p. 112.
46. Ibid., p. 114.
47. Ibid., pp. 122–3.
48. Ibid., p. 125.
49. Ibid., p. 116.
50. Montesquieu, *The Spirit of the Laws*, trans. Thomas Nugent (New York: Hafner Publishing Company, 1949), chap. XI, esp. p. 163.
51. Tocqueville, *The Recollections of Alexis de Tocqueville*, trans. Teixeira de Mattos, ed. J. P. Mayer (Cleveland: The World Publishing Company, 1959), p. 201.

Chapter Three

1. Martin Diamond and Louis Smith have both recognized that Tocqueville's section on administrative decentralization and federalism is extremely important for Tocqueville's aim to diffuse the debased taste for equality. They do not conclude, as I do, that the purpose of this section is to show why institutional arrangements cannot provide the whole solution, and that, thus, Part I leads towards Part II as the necessary next step in the argument. cf. Martin Diamond, "The Ends of Federalism," *Publius* 3 (Fall 1973), Volume 3, pp. 129–52. cf. also Louis Smith, "Alexis de Tocqueville and Public Administration," *Public Administration Review* 1942, no. 2, p. 221.
2. Tocqueville, *Democracy in America*, p. 157.
3. Ibid., p. 159.
4. Ibid., p. 160.
5. Ibid.
6. Ibid., p. 161.
7. Ibid., p. 162.
8. Ibid., pp. 162–3.
9. Ibid., p. 161.
10. Ibid., pp. 163–4–5.
11. Ibid., p. 164.
12. Ibid.

13. James Madison, *The Federalist*, no. 10, Clinton Rossiter ed. (New York: The New American Library, Inc., Mentor Books, 1964).

14. Tocqueville, *Democracy in America*, p. 164.

15. Ibid., p. 166.

16. Ibid., p. 167.

17. Ibid.

18. Ibid.

19. Ibid., p. 170.

20. Ibid., pp. 171–3.

21. Ibid., p. 173.

22. Ibid.

23. Walter Berns, *Freedom, Virtue, and the First Amendment*, (New York: Greenwood Press, 1969), and *The First Amendment and the Future of American Democracy* (New York: Basic Books, Inc., 1976).

24. For a serious and also funny illustration of this, consider Kenneth Kolson's delightful description of the intellectual confusions of Federal Communications Commissioner Nicholas Johnson. Kenneth Kolson, "Broadcasting in the Public Interest: The Legacy of Communications Commissioner Nicholas Johnson," *The Administrative Law Review* 30 (Winter 1978), pp. 133–65.

25. Berns, *The First Amendment*, p. 169.

26. Tocqueville, *Democracy in America*, p. 174.

27. Ibid., p. 177.

28. Ibid., p. 176.

29. Ibid.

30. Ibid., p. 178.

31. Ibid., p. 179.

32. Ibid., p. 176.

33. Ibid., p. 177.

34. Ibid., p. 181.

35. Ibid., pp. 182–3, 186–92.

36. Ibid., p. 191.

37. Ibid., p. 184.

38. Ibid., p. 206.

39. Ibid., p. 207.

40. Ibid., p. 214.

41. Ibid., cf. also p. 231.

42. Ibid., pp. 217–19.

43. Ibid., p. 342.

44. Ibid., p. 226.

45. Ibid., p. 233, n. 4.

46. Ibid., p. 233.

47. Ibid.

48. Ibid., p. 232.

49. Ibid., p. 234.

50. Ibid.

51. Ibid., p. 241.

52. Ibid., p. 252.

53. Ibid., p. 244.

54. Ibid., p. 696, (Tocqueville's note "K" to p. 87).
55. Ibid., p. 248.
56. Ibid., p. 255.
57. Ibid.
58. Ibid., p. 283.
59. Ibid, pp. 256–63.
60. Ibid., p. 283.
61. Ibid., p. 269.
62. Ibid., p. 265.
63. Ibid.
64. Ibid., p. 266. I think this quotation damages Doris Goldstein's thesis that Tocqueville's own political values are compatable with Catholicism. cf. Doris Goldstein, *Trial of Faith* (New York: Scientific Publishing Company, Inc., 1975).
65. Ibid., p. 269.
66. Ibid., p. 273.
67. Ibid., p. 275.
68. Ibid., p. 273.
69. Ibid., p. 275–6.
70. Rousseau, *The Social Contract*, pp. 204–223. The official contentlessness of the civil religion is like the contentlessness of the general will. What happens is that in its spiritual life the general will senses its own existence but not *as* its own existence; it, therefore, worships itself as God.
71. Ibid., p. 223.
72. Tocqueville, *Democracy in America*, pp. 284–5.
73. Niccolo Machiavelli, *The Discourses*, in *The Prince and the Discourses*, Max Lerner, ed., Christian E. Detmold, trans. (New York: Random House, Inc., 1950), pp. 227–8.

Chapter Four

1. Tocqueville, *Democracy in America*, p. 291.
2. Ibid., p. 302.
3. Ibid., pp. 297–8, 301.
4. Ibid., p. 296.
5. Ibid., p. 311.
6. Ibid., p. 312, n. 29.
7. Ibid., p. 297.
8. Ibid., p. 300, n. 8.
9. Ibid., pp. 306–7, n. 19.
10. Ibid., p. 314.
11. Ibid., p. 315.
12. Ibid., p. 317.
13. Ibid., pp. 319–21.
14. Ibid., p. 331.
15. Ibid.
16. Ibid., p. 314, n. 32.
17. Ibid., p. 339.
18. Ibid., p. 342.

19. Ibid.
20. Ibid., p. 345.
21. Ibid., p. 362.
22. Ibid.
23. Rousseau, *Social Contract*, pp. 152–3, and following.
24. Ibid., p. 78.
25. Tocqueville, *Democracy in America*, p. 369.

Chapter Five

   1. J. P. Mayer notes this in his book, *Alexis de Tocqueville, A Biographical Study in Political Science* (New York: Harper and Brothers, 1960), pp. 117–8.
   2. Tocqueville, *Democracy in America*, p. 383.
   3. Ibid., pp. 157, and chapter 8, Part II, esp. pp. 231–4.
   4. Ibid., pp. 342–3.
   5. Ibid., p. 11.
   6. Ibid., p. 393.
   7. Ibid., p. 84.
   8. Ibid., p. 396.
   9. Ibid., pp. 398–9.
  10. Ibid., p. 399.
  11. Ibid.
  12. Ibid., p. 400.
  13. Ibid.
  14. Ibid., p. 401.
  15. I think that Mill himself did not see this important point in his review of *Democracy in America*. Mill finds in Tocqueville support for his own concern that individuality and creative variety are being threatened in modern society. But he disagrees with Tocqueville in that, whereas Tocqueville attributes this evil to the displacement of the aristocratic class by the democratic class, Mill thinks that the evil consists in the fact that one class does exercise intellectual dominion. Mill reads Tocqueville as joining his own thought that modern commercialism has bred a universal bourgeoise mentality that threatens intellectual freedom. He has misgivings with Tocqueville for having devoted so much attention to the particularly dem7ocratic character of the modern tyrant; to Mill that seems incidental. To put this in other words, Mill is primarily interested in intellectual freedom; he wants to defend that value against any and all forms of oppression, whether it be modern and relatively subtle forms or pre-modern and crude ones. Therefore when Tocqueville makes his discussion of intellectual freedom serve his broader aim of comparing and contrasting the democratic and the aristocratic regimes, Mill will not follow.
  That Mill did not take up the question of the regime seriously, as Tocqueville did, is one way of explaining the problem with Mill's thought altogether. Mill leaves himself nothing to do but to exhort, to whomever enjoys intellectual influence, to be tolerant of ideas that seem strange. And even though in his *On Liberty* Mill expresses that exhortation as eloquently as it might be expressed, he is not able to escape the irony of his position. *On Liberty* reads as a brief for the equality of

all opinions before the authority of the public; but as we observe with Tocqueville, that attitude is precisely the one by which democracy limits intellectual activity.

16. Tocqueville, *Democracy in America*, p. 403.
17. Ibid., pp. 403–4.
18. Ibid., p. 404.
19. Ibid., p. 402.
20. Ibid., p. 409.
21. Ibid., p. 413.
22. Ibid., pp. 412–13.
23. Ibid., p. 417.
24. Ibid., p. 415.
25. Ibid., pp. 415–6.
26. cf. p. 6 of this chapter, *supra*.
27. Tocqueville, *Democracy in America*, p. 417.
28. Ibid., pp. 419–20.
29. Ibid., p. 420.
30. Ibid., p. 518.
31. Ibid., p. 425.
32. Ibid., p. 422.
33. Ibid., p. 425.
34. Ibid., p. 426–31.
35. Ibid., p. 429.
36. Ibid., p. 430.
37. Ibid.
38. Ibid., p. 426.
39. Ibid., p. 428.
40. Ibid., p. 430.
41. Ibid., p. 434.
42. Ibid., p. 435.
43. Ibid.
44. Ibid., p. 436.
45. Ibid., p. 456.
46. Ibid., p. 450.
47. Ibid.
48. Ibid., p. 464.
49. Ibid., p. 440.
50. Ibid., pp. 453–4.
51. Ibid., p. 454.
52. Ibid., p. 455.
53. Compare Tocqueville's judgment of the effects of the theater in democracy to what Rousseau says about censorship generally, in the *Social Contract*, and his thoughts on the theater in his letter to D'Alembert, published under the title, *Jean-Jacques Rousseau, Politics and the Arts*, ed. and trans. Allan Bloom (Ithaca: Cornell University Press, 1968).
54. Tocqueville, *Democracy in America*, p. 461.
55. Ibid., p. 460–1.
56. Ibid., p. 469.

Chapter Six

1. Tocqueville, *Democracy in America*, p. 471. It seems to me that from a more classical perspective Tocqueville's discussions of the effects of a democracy on beliefs and on habits (mores) is readily understandable, but his devoting a full book to "feelings" would seem odd. Is it not the case that how one feels about certain things is simply a function of how our natural passions are allowed to express themselves through the structure of our beliefs and habits? Why then is the theme of "feelings" separated from the themes of beliefs and habits discussed on a par with them? This question obviously cannot be answered except by reading Book 2, but I think it is tempting to speculate in a general way that Tocqueville's devoting a separate discussion to "feelings" is prepared for by Rousseau's having made *sentiment* the ultimate authority by which man knows his existence; i.e. not Descartes' *"cogito"* but rather *"je sens"* is the key to man's human awareness. In other words, the contemporary reader is prepared to accept a book on sentiments because we are somehow interested in the way that different social conditions either stifle or put us in touch with the sentiment of existence.

2. Ibid., p. 402.
3. Ibid., pp. 473–6.
4. Ibid., pp. 477–8.
5. Ibid., p. 478.
6. Ibid., p. 649.
7. Ibid., p. 474.
8. Ibid., pp. 474–6.
9. Ibid., p. 473.
10. Ibid., p. 475, cf. p. 643.
11. Ibid., pp. 477–8.
12. Ibid., pp. 479–80.
13. Ibid., p. 483.
14. Ibid., p. 485.
15. Ibid.
16. Ibid., p. 489.
17. Ibid., p. 491.
18. Ibid., p. 493.
19. Ibid., p. 492.
20. Ibid., p. 493.
21. Ibid., p. 494.
22. Ibid., p. 498.
23. Ibid.
24. Ibid., p. 501.
25. Ibid., p. 505.
26. Ibid., p. 506.
27. Ibid., p. 509.

28. Marvin Zetterbaum recognizes that Tocqueville thinks it necessary that democratic citizens feel and act on motives fundamentally different from self-interest. But he holds that Tocqueville thought that they could acquire nobler motives through the operation of self-interest. Distinguishing Tocqueville from Madison, Zetterbaum says, "The democratic desires Tocqueville has in mind must

make men moral, that is, must make them citizens. In the extreme, these devices would make them selfless. Ironically, they pursue this end by relying on self-interest, albeit self-interest rightly understood." I think Zetterbaum in effect charges Tocqueville with something more severe than irony. I argue that what *is* ironic is that Americans interpret their own natural capacity for acts of kindness and helpfulness *as if* it were dictated by self-interest. If Tocqueville were to say that Americans are actually motivated by self-interest, but in such a way that they transcend self-interest, that would be not only irony but contradiction. cf. Zetterbaum, *Tocqueville and the Problem of Democracy*, p. 90.

29. Tocqueville, *Democracy in America*, p. 49.

30. Ibid., p. 513.

31. cf. my comment on the concluding passages of the final chapter of volume I, p. 113 *supra*.

32. Ibid., p. 516.

33. Ibid.

34. Ibid., p. 518.

35. Ibid., p. 420.

36. Ibid., pp. 520–1.

37. I have already mentioned Seymour Drescher in this context. cf. Drescher, *Tocqueville and England*, p. 200.

38. Tocqueville, *Democracy in America*, p. 529.

39. Ibid., p. 530.

40. Ibid.

41. The comment is from a letter from Tocqueville to the Comtesse de Pisieux, quoted by Max Beloff in his article, "Tocqueville et l'Angleterre," in *Livre du Centenaire, 1859–1959* (Paris: Centre National de la Recherche Scientifique, 1960), p. 100.

Chapter Seven

1. Tocqueville, *Democracy in America*, p. 535.

2. Ibid., p. 538. cf. J. J. Rousseau, *Emile*, trans. Barbara Foxley, (London: J. M. Dent and Sons Ltd., 1966), pp. 190–91.

3. Ibid., p. 539.

4. Aristotle, *Nichomachean Ethics*, trans. Martin Ostwald (Indianapolis: The Bobbs-Merrill Company, Inc., 1962), p. 43.

5. Tocqueville, *Democracy in America*, p. 543.

6. Ibid., p. 542.

7. Ibid., p. 543.

8. Ibid., p. 544.

9. Ibid., p. 551.

10. Ibid., p. 561.

11. Ibid., p. 560.

12. Ibid., p. 562.

13. Ibid., p. 565.

14. Ibid., p. 566.

15. Ibid., pp. 566–7.

16. Rousseau, *Emile*, p. 337.

17. Ibid.

18. Ibid.

19. Tocqueville, *Democracy in America*, p. 568.

20. I think Rousseau suggests this by the fact that he spends much less time outlining Sophy's education than Emile's. Sophy's education is easier than Emile's because her selfhood is less precariously dependent on the illusion whereby sexuality blooms into love. This suggestion tends to be confirmed by Rousseau's indication that whereas Emile is a fictitious character, Sophy was an actual girl that he knew. op. cit. p. 365.

21. Tocqueville, *Democracy in America*, p. 571.

22. Ibid., p. 571, n. 1.

23. Ibid., pp. 572–3.

24. Ibid., pp. 574–5.

25. Ibid., p. 579.

26. Ibid., p. 576.

27. Ibid., p. 576.

28. Ibid., p. 574–5.

29. Plato, *Republic*, trans. Allan Bloom (New York: Basic Books, Inc., 1968), p. 253.

30. Tocqueville appears to accept the implications of Rousseau's statement, which contrasts with the more traditional view, that, "there is no original sin in the human heart, . . . The only natural passion is self-love or selfishness taken in a wider sense. [This] self-love only becomes good or bad by the use made of it and the relations established by its means." Rousseau, *Emile*, p. 56.

31. Tocqueville, *Democracy in America*, p. 584.

32. Ibid., p. 582.

33. Ibid., p. 584.

34. Ibid.

35. Ibid., pp. 586–7.

36. Ibid., pp. 588–9.

37. Ibid., p. 589.

38. Ibid.

39. Ibid., p. 592, n. 1.

40. Ibid., p. 594.

41. Ibid., p. 595.

42. Ibid., p. 598.

43. Ibid., p. 598 and following.

44. Ibid., p. 598.

45. Ibid.

46. Ibid.

47. Ibid., p. 601.

48. Ibid., p. 602.

49. Ibid.

50. Ibid.

51. Ibid.

52. Ibid. The Lawrence translation of the concluding passages of chapter 18 is misleading on this point. Lawrence translates, "as such differences become less [the notion of honor] grows feeble; and when they disappear, it will vanish too."

But the French is conditional, "*et il disparaitrait avec elles.*" Honor *would* vanish in a universal society, but Tocqueville is not predicting that that must come. cf. Tocqueville, *De la Democratie en Amerique* (London: Macmillan & Co., 1961), p. 247.

53. Ibid., p. 454.

54. Ibid., p. 607.

55. Ibid., p. 610.

56. Ibid., p. 613.

57. Ibid., p. 613.

58. Ibid., p. 619.

59. Ibid., p. 625.

60. Ibid., p. 621.

61. Ibid., p. 624.

62. N. Machiavelli, *The Prince*, trans. Lugi Ricci, in *The Prince and the Discourses*, ed. Max Lerner (New York: The Modern Library, 1950), esp. chapters 12 and 13.

63. Tocqueville, *Democracy in America*, p. 629.

64. Ibid., pp. 625, 629.

65. Ibid., pp. 632–3.

66. Ibid., p. 634.

67. cf. Machiavelli, *Discourses*, in *The Prince and the Discourses*, trans. Christian E. Detmold, bk. I, chap. 19. Note that Machiavelli is referred to by name in this section of *Democracy in America*.

68. Tocqueville, *Democracy in America*, pp. 634–5.

Chapter Eight

1. Tocqueville, *Democracy in America*, pp. 12, 284.

2. Ibid., p. 49.

3. Ibid., p. 123.

4. Tocqueville, *Recollections*, pp. 223–4.

5. Ibid., pp. 224–5.

6. Tocqueville, *The European Revolution*, p. 146.

Index